by Benjamin B. Tregoe
John W. Zimmerman

Top Management Strategy

What It Is and How to Make It Work

SIMON AND SCHUSTER NEW YORK

Copyright © 1980 by Kepner-Tregoe, Inc.
First Touchstone edition 1983
A Touchstone Book
Published by Simon & Schuster, Inc.
Simon & Schuster Building
Rockefeller Center
1230 Avenue of the Americas
New York, New York 10020

TOUCHSTONE and colophon are registered trademarks
of Simon & Schuster, Inc.
Manufactured in the United States of America
5 6 7 8 9 10
5 6 7 8 9 10 Pbk.

Library of Congress Cataloging in Publication Data

Tregoe, Benjamin B
Top management strategy.

Bibliography: p.
Includes index.
1. Industrial management.   2. Corporate
planning.   I. Zimmerman, John W., joint author.
II. Title.
HD31.T683   658.4′012   80-15819
ISBN 0-671-25401-4
ISBN 0-671-25402-2 Pbk.

Acknowledgments

This book owes its existence to the top managers who have trusted us with their most important possession: the strategy of their organization. We owe them an immense debt both for having confidence in us and for contributing to our understanding of what strategy is and how it can be set and implemented. Beyond this experience in strategy setting and implementation, many of these top executives have also given us substantial time for in-depth, follow-up interviews. We owe them special thanks. Our work on strategy formulation has been carried out through the Kepner-Tregoe Strategy Group, a division of Kepner-Tregoe, Inc. We are indebted to all our colleagues in this group for providing us with insights and examples based on their experiences as strategy practitioners. We are also grateful to Peter Tobia, editor of the manuscript, and to those top managers and professional associates who reviewed earlier drafts of this work.

Contents

Foreword

When I was a child, I recall stopping to watch a game being played by a number of teenagers. I impatiently asked my parents, "What are they doing?" I was too young to figure out what was taking place before me. "They are playing ice hockey," I was told. Once the ground rules of the game were explained, the seemingly random movements of the players fell into place. The movements made sense. My parents had given me something useful: An idea that organized the experience.

The book that Ben Tregoe and John Zimmerman have written brings to mind this half-forgotten incident. This is a book that makes sense of all the diverse activities of a business organization. It provides a clear idea of what it means to think and manage strategically. Key managers who read this book will know pretty quickly whether or not they and their organization are strategically focused. They will also better understand the fundamentals of strategic management from the formulation to the implementation of strategy.

This volume presents a unique perspective and a dynamic new concept. It contends that strategy and long-range planning must be separated. This flies in the face of much of the prevailing wisdom. The significance of the "Driving Force" as a concept to clarify strategic options is the authors' major contribution to strategic thinking. The Driving Force is an impartial method for putting competing points of view on the table and ultimately for gaining consensus on the organization's future strategy.

In my own company, Cargill Inc., one of the largest privately held companies in the world and certainly among the most complex organizationally, the concept of Driving Force was a key to gaining clarity about our strategic direction.

So the book is a solidly practical one. There is a welcome absence of diagrams, flowcharts and all the other mickey-mouse of theoretical undertakings. The book is based on first-hand experience. The points that are made are amplified by a large number of examples drawn from the authors' practical experience. Included are some experiences from Cargill.

Finally, the book is short. Here at last is a book with a substantial message that can be read in one sitting. Good reading!

WHITNEY MACMILLAN
Chairman
Cargill Incorporated
Minneapolis, Minnesota

Preface

This book is the result of research conducted not in the library but on the firing line. Since 1971, we have been exploring strategy formulation with senior executives in more than two hundred major organizations around the world. They range in size from fifteen million to fifteen billion dollars in volume and span both the private and public sectors. In more than one hundred of these organizations we have helped top executives set their future strategy.

Though we would like to say that all our consulting experiences were stellar performances, there have been rough spots, particularly at the outset of our work. We have learned from our successes and mistakes. And this book is based on both.

Throughout, we have used a wide number of examples drawn from our on-the-job experience. While "naming names" makes for exciting copy, such exposure would violate client confidentiality. Consequently, we have camouflaged the examples, but have remained true to the basic facts.

This book is aimed at senior managers who are concerned with the direction of their organizations. It is about strategy formulation and *not* long-range planning. It will present ideas to be read, thought about, discussed and then acted upon. Our purpose in writing it is to: *define* the meaning of strategy; *analyze* the concept of the "Driving Force," the key to strategic thinking; *describe* how an organization can integrate its strategy with its operations; and finally, *provoke* top managers to improve their strategic thinking. We expect that our readers will better be able to evaluate critically the quality of their own strategic thinking and to assess the effectiveness of their organizations' efforts to set strategy. They should finish this book with a good grasp of what strategy is, how it relates to long-range planning and operations, and some key ideas for formulating strategy in their own organizations, along with our guidelines for implementing it.

In today's business world more and more women are moving into top positions in all organizations. This is as it should be. But in writing this book we have found it cumbersome to continually make references to "he or she," so we have used the masculine personal pronoun throughout and hope our readers understand that limitations of style rather than male chauvinism dictated it.

We have written for executives with little spare time, but enough time to spare to think about their organizations' futures. It is a straightforward book which requires no elaborate road map.

Top Management Strategy

CHAPTER ONE

Strategy and Survival

AT THE CROSSROADS

Whether you are a chief executive officer, a member of the top corporate management team, or a key divisional executive, you no doubt have grappled with the question: Where should my organization be headed? Simple and straightforward as this question is, we have seen many top managers puzzled, perplexed and even deeply troubled trying to answer it, and with good reason. Put this question to yourself and your top management team and you put your organization on trial. For the question cuts to the nature and purpose of the organization, to your vision of what the organization should become. It is a question about your corporate strategy.

Trying to answer this deceptively simple question about corporate strategy leads to more specific questions: What is a strategy? How is strategy different from and related to long-range planning and operational decision making? What determines the scope of products* and markets? What are the future strategic options? How do these compare with where the organization is headed now? How does top management make sure that strategy drives the operations of the business? Answering these questions calls for a clear definition of strategy and a concept for setting it. And that is what you will find in these pages.

These questions about where an organization should be headed

---

* In a service organization the "services" offered are its "products." Thus, the words product and service are synonymous. Throughout this book we will use the word "products" to describe what an organization offers to the markets it serves.

15

are challenging. They assume that no matter how strong an organization's present position, the status quo is always on trial. It is always subject to comparison with our expectations about what we want the organization to be. And these questions assume that man makes the organization he serves. They put the destiny of the organization squarely where it belongs: not in the hands of the gods but in the hands and heads of the key executives who guide it.

STRATEGY DEFINED

To understand what strategy is and how it relates to the operating side of the business, consider two facets which are critical to the survival of all organizations: *what* the organization wants to be and *how* it should get there. While both these facets are integral to long-range thinking, they must not be confused. An organization's future self-definition—what it wants to be—and its planning and operational decision making—how it gets there—are related but separate dimensions. Since what an organization wants to be sets direction, it must be formulated prior to long-range planning and the day-to-day decision making that follows from such planning.

Unfortunately, the word "strategy" has been used rather casually both in the literature on the subject and in the marketplace. In fact, it has assumed a variety of meanings, some of which confuse the *what* and *how* dimensions. Managers talk frequently about "our pricing strategy," "our manpower strategy," or "our financial strategy." Such "strategies," in our view, are really major operational decision points which presume a clear understanding of what the organization wants to be. They are related to *how* an organization will realize its future self-definition or vision.

In a similar fashion, strategy is sometimes called strategic planning and is then used interchangeably with long-range planning. For example, one book entitled *Strategic Planning Systems* proclaims on the front cover that it "explains the long-range planning process."* In this instance, strategy, again, is related to the *how*. In other instances, top managers use the word strategy to mean the

---

* Peter Lorange and Richard F. Vancil, *Strategic Planning Systems*. (Englewood Cliffs, New Jersey: Prentice-Hall, Inc., 1977)

nature and direction of the organization, its basic purpose. This is how we use the term.

We are not interested in legislating the meaning of such an important word as strategy. However, to successfully set strategy, you must have a clear understanding of what strategy is and of what constitutes the end product of strategy formulation. Strategy should provide a picture of the organization as it wants to look in the future. Strategy is vision directed· at *what* the organization should be, and not *how* the organization will get there. We define strategy as *the framework which guides those choices that determine the nature and direction of an organization.* Those choices relate to the scope of an organization's products or services, markets, key capabilities, growth, return, and allocation of resources.

STRATEGY . . . IT'S A MATTER OF WHO

Every organization has a momentum or direction. It is headed somewhere. Top managers who do not consciously set strategy risk having their organization's momentum or direction developed implicitly, haphazardly or by others inside or outside the organization. This point is critically important and frequently overlooked. Having your direction set by default can mean that it is set by those down the line, or by government, banks, competition, labor unions and so on.

For example, take the experience of one company that enjoyed so much success with a specialized product that the president was approached about the prospects of taking his company public. Investment bankers made the prospect look appealing.

As plans moved along for a public underwriting, the very basis of the company's success proved a problem. The company manufactured and held a strong position in the stereo market with a single, widely accepted product. Investment counselors felt this single-product position would project as a weakness in the stock market. Accordingly, the president was encouraged to develop and introduce a series of other products for the same marketplace.

The new products never took hold. When the company retrenched and concentrated on its established strengths, growth picked up again. The president found it did not pay to let the investment community dictate his company's direction.

Laws, policies or regulations from governmental entities may have the effect of determining an organization's future direction whether or not a conscious strategy exists. Those top managers who clearly set strategy can use their insight about the government as an input to that strategy. Those organizations that do not have a conscious strategy or do not reassess their strategy periodically merely react to government actions. Their direction is set by whatever threat or opportunity they happen to be avoiding or pursuing.

Thus, government regulations and warnings about the hazards of cigarette smoking have fundamentally changed the direction of many of the major tobacco companies in the U.S. These companies have responded to the hostile environment by scrambling to diversify—acquiring businesses ranging from brewing to oil production to food processing. The president of R.J. Reynolds Industries, Inc., summed up his organization's ten-year diversification effort: "The company evolved as a holding company with no direct management from the top."*

Sometimes direction can be set by a number of levels and functions in an organization. One company is an independent distributor serving a geographic market for a manufacturer of heavy construction equipment. The organization was literally being pulled apart by a number of diverse activities, some proposed, some in the process of implementation. The V.P. of Operations was seriously considering broadening and extending his organization's maintenance activities by adding the capability to maintain competitors' equipment. Meanwhile, the V.P. of Finance moved toward establishing the organization's substantial credit function as a basis for another business. The V.P. of Sales had a well-trained and highly motivated sales force, but felt the product line needed enrichment. He was interested in adding basic and support equipment to his product line that was made by other manufacturers. As if all this were not enough, it was production's job to meet the specialized needs of its customers by customizing attachments for certain vehicles. This required considerable skill which the director of production wanted to sell to other businesses.

While each of these managers can be complimented for taking

* "When Marketing Takes Over At R.J. Reynolds," *Business Week,* November 13, 1978, p. 82.

initiative in a corporate strategic vacuum, their activities had the potential to change significantly the direction of the business. Some of the outcomes could have had serious implications for the distributor's legal agreement with his manufacturer. Others would have splintered the efforts of the organization without any conscious corporate decision to do so. Fortunately, a corporate strategy was developed before these "functional directions" proceeded too far. This organization could have paid a high price for having its direction determined by separate decisions in a variety of places and levels.

We are not saying that the managers in the above examples are any less capable than other managers. Nor are we saying that strategy is a panacea for every difficulty. However, managers who have a keen sense of where their organization should be headed are much more resistant to either "shotgunning" or compromising the choices that will get them there.

ADAPTING FOR SURVIVAL

Those who have avoided coming to terms with the "what/how" separation have not necessarily doomed their organizations to failure. In a sense, organizations are like living organisms. They must adapt to survive. Some organizations have been able to adapt by focusing primarily on present operations. These organizations face the future by continually improving operating effectiveness. They are action-prone and go for the operational fix: capital expenditure expansion or delays, hiring limitations, tighter inventory control, increasing or reducing staff services, price changes, more efficient delivery systems, and the like. While information about the future is important for these organizations, it is used mainly to set limits on the expansion of current operations.

But the operations palliative, if taken alone, is dangerous medicine for treating a crisis or change which could threaten the survival of the business. If an organization is headed in the wrong direction, the last thing it needs is to get there more efficiently. And if an organization is headed in the right direction, it surely does not need to have that direction unwittingly changed by operational action taken in a strategic void.

Other organizations adapt for survival in a different way. They recognize the critical importance of efficient operations but they know that operational activities must be guided by a well-defined strategy. They do not assume current operations as a given for the future but ask: What's happening in the world around us? What does that suggest about our current direction? What should be our future product and market scope? These organizations would use information regarding the future to answer these questions of strategy and not merely to project current operations forward. They know that to survive in an environment of turbulent change, operational planning must proceed within the framework of their strategy. Once their strategy is set, it guides operational decisions.

THE STRATEGY/OPERATIONS RELATIONSHIP

The relationship between strategy and operations can be illustrated in the following way:

WHAT / HOW	STRATEGY	
	Clear ⬇	**Unclear** ⬇
OPERATIONS **Effective** ➡	**I** Clear strategy and effective operations have equaled success in the past and will in the future	**II** Unclear strategy but effective operations have equaled success in the past, but success is doubtful in the future
Ineffective ➡	**III** Clear strategy but ineffective operations have sometimes worked in the past in the short run, but increasing competition makes success doubtful in the future	**IV** Unclear strategy and ineffective operations have equaled failure in the past and will in the future

In these four quadrants we can see that with clear strategy and effective operations we will invariably win. With unclear strategy and ineffective operations we will always lose. If the strategy is clear but the operations are ineffective, the result is in question. We may still win, but now winning depends almost totally on our ability to predict and then be carried by the kindness of external forces such as the economy and competition—forces not generally known for their beneficence. Similarly, if operations are effective but the strategy is unclear, we may survive by being swept forward efficiently. But for how long?

The W. T. Grant Co. is a vivid example of a company in quadrant IV. It was a "loser" because it did not have a clear idea of *what* it should be in the future, and also because it had inadequate operational plans. The following commentaries from *Business Week* attest to Grant's lack of direction:

> Worse yet, early on Grant seemingly could not make up its mind what kind of store it was. "There was a lot of dissension within the company whether we should go the K-Mart route or go after the Ward's and Penney position," says a former executive. "Ed Staley and Lou Lustenberger were at loggerheads over the issue, with the upshot being we took a position between the two and that consequently stood for nothing." *

In addition to lacking direction, Grant's day-to-day operations were ineffective:

> From 1963 to 1973 Grant opened 612 stores and expanded 91 others, with the bulk of the increase starting in 1968 under the guidance of President Richard W. Mayer and Chairman Edward Staley.
>
> "The expansion program placed a great strain on the physical and human capability of the company to cope with the program," says Kendrick. "These were all large stores we were opening—6 million to 7 million square feet per year—and the expansion of our management organization just did not match the expansion of our stores." Adds a former operations executive: "Our training program couldn't keep up with the explosion of stores, and it didn't take long for the mediocrity to begin to show." †

* "How W. T. Grant lost $175-million last year," *Business Week,* February 24, 1975, p. 75.

† *Ibid.*

In the quadrant I, The General Electric Co. is typical of a "winner." With a clear image of what it should be in the future, it has also been eminently successful in its operations. Sears Roebuck & Co. is another organization that, over the years, has consistently demonstrated the ability to anticipate changes, to set direction and to organize quickly and efficiently to move in that direction.† However, Sears has had strategic difficulties in the recent past,‡ and may have shifted from quadrant I to quadrant II.

In quadrants II and III, we will probably find the majority of organizations. Some companies, for example, those founded on the strength of a technological breakthrough, can be placed in quadrant III. With a clear sense of strategy by virtue of an invention or innovation, operations may lag behind. Shakeouts within an industry then occur as competition intensifies and as operationally ineffective companies find that breakthroughs can take them only so far. This has been the trend in the semi-conductor industry. A company such as Texas Instruments is a "winner" because, unlike many companies in that industry, it has moved to quadrant I, a tribute to its clear strategy and its effective operations.

The Swiss watch industry is representative of quadrant II. Superbly efficient at producing and marketing, the industry seemed unable to adapt to changes in technology. In the U.S., strong operations have been historically more important than clear strategic thinking. In the past, many U.S. organizations have been in quadrant II and survived even though they lacked a clear sense of strategic direction. After all, with unlimited resources, skilled labor, a large and homogeneous market, and world-wide demand for U.S. products, who needed to think much about what kind of business they wanted to be in the future?

Now, however, with diminishing resources, world competition, and increasing intervention by governments and other special interest groups, even the most efficient operations may no longer survive the handicap of a lack of clear strategic direction. Today's company must formulate a clear strategy from which flows effective operations.

---

† For a concise summary of the history of Sears, Roebuck & Co., see Alfred D. Chandler, Jr., *Strategy and Structure* (Cambridge, MA: MIT Press, 1962), pp. 225–282.

‡ "Can Sears Come Back?," *Dun's Review*, February 1979, p. 68.

STRATEGY VERSUS LONG-RANGE PLANNING:
CLEARING UP THE CONFUSION

From our work with top management on strategy formulation, we have seen a dominant theme appear with disturbing regularity: the confusion between strategic thinking and long-range planning and the adverse impact on strategy formulation. We have already explored the need to separate strategy from operations. While this separation is easy to grasp intellectually, it is often blurred in practice. In our view, an inappropriate understanding of the role of long-range planning is the primary cause for this blurring and the resulting confusion.

To clear this up, strategy and long-range planning must be separated. Why? Many organizations, after all, have long-range plans; many top managers are convinced that such plans fulfill the need for a strategy. Why, then, can't long-range planning be used to set strategy? What is there about long-range planning that makes it inadequate?

Our intent in making the following points is to show why long-range planning is inadequate for strategy formulation. It is not to debunk or belittle long-range planning. This is a necessary and useful tool, but as with any tool, it is effective only when used for its proper purpose. Letting long-range planning set your strategy is very much like choosing an excellent course of action to treat an incorrectly diagnosed problem. Here is why:

1. Long-range plans tend to be based on projections of current operations into the future. While long-range plans are frequently developed with a recognition of economic, environmental, socio-political and technological changes, such inputs are used chiefly to determine how expansive or cautious the organization should be about projecting its current operations. These inputs tend not to be used as a basis for determining a strategic direction. As one example, the V.P. of Operations and a Director of a major company had this to say:

When I came into this position, I had to develop a business plan. I found that the way plans were put together was to use a trendline approach. The senior people who assembled the plan said that our growth rate for the past several years had been between four and six percent, so that should be the type of growth rate in the future. One of our products had averaged 32% growth per year in one geographical area. They just assumed the same growth rate in the future. Two things were missing in this straight-lining a variable into the future. There was a technical flaw, in that a multitude of variables were simply ignored. More important, the plans lacked a long-term sense of direction and value. They didn't address the issue of where we wanted to go.

Typical example or exception? Whichever, it does illustrate the weakness of long-range planning as a substitute for setting strategy. Long-range planning does not invite managers to think strategically, to think about what the organization should be. Put differently, arriving at the future by long-range planning simply does not encourage managers to command their organization's future.

2. The extrapolation from the present mentioned above occurs despite many of the writings in the field which urge the establishment of objectives up-front as a part of long-range planning. In fact, many managers do not set objectives which define their future because they lack an approach to assist them. They are forced to build their future on the foundation of the projections rather than on a clear definition of what they want their organization to be. Using this approach, the plans which companies make determine their direction, rather than a clear sense of direction determining their plans.

3. Where long-range objectives do exist to guide planning, they are invariably set in financial terms. Once set, projections for products, markets and resources are then developed to achieve these objectives. But who gives attention to the fundamental *strategic* question: What determines the future scope of the organization's products and markets? While every organization has financial objectives around which it plans and measures its operations, few organizations use

such objectives as the primary determinant of their product and market scope. When long-range financial objectives are used as the primary lead for long-range planning, they can pre-empt critical considerations of what determines product and market scope, the resources to be put in place to support that product and market scope, and the expected results to be achieved. Typically, long-range financial objectives are set, plans are formulated and these key strategic issues are put to rest without ever being examined.

4. Long-range plans are built up from the lowest levels, where information exists to make projections. These projections from various parts of the organization are consolidated and, in total, become the recommended plan. By the time these accumulated and detailed plans reach the top, there is virtually no opportunity for injecting fresh insight about the future. In fact, top management's ability to modify these plans, except in minor ways, can be severely hampered. If top managers do not have a clear strategy with which to assess the plans that percolate up from the organization, they become locked into allocating resources on the basis of these plans. Flexibility is gone. The comment of one chief executive immersed in the planning cycle is typical: ''By the time we get through with our long-range planning cycle, we are all so engrossed in the precision of our projections that we have lost our ability to question whether they are taking us where we want to go.''

5. Long-range plans invariably tend to be overly optimistic. This results primarily from the desire of those making the projections at various levels of the organization to do better in their respective areas in the years ahead. This optimism tends to exist in the weaker areas of organizations as well as in the stronger, thereby blurring distinctions between the two which are vital for the efficient allocation of resources on a strategic basis. By the time this optimism reaches top management, every unit has predicted that given ''x'' amount of new resources, it will do ''y'' amount better in the year ahead. One executive put it this way. ''If you work something like sales forecasts from the bottom up, you're

going to end up with far more optimistic sales projections than you could ever realize, simply because you compound the areas of optimism as you go up the ladder." This further restricts the freedom of top management to make changes, for such projections become the prevailing corporate wisdom. Any changes made that are not purely perfunctory appear as arbitrary and capricious to the rest of the organization. Since the allocation of resources is tied to these optimistic plans, the persuasiveness of strong personalities and the unrealistic goals they guarantee to reach often undermine strategic considerations.

6. Long-range planning usually begins with assumptions about the environment—the economy, technological change, socio-political events—and the organization's strengths and weaknesses. Though this information could have great strategic significance, long-range planning tends to utilize such data basically as a guide for determining how optimistic or pessimistic to make the long-range product and market projections. This is so because long-range planning is not a process which enables critical data about the external environment to be used for strategic purposes.

7. Long-range plans tend to be inflexible (even though they are usually presented in three-ring binders as evidence of their flexibility). It takes a tremendous amount of work to project three years ahead, let alone five years and beyond. Without a clear strategic framework to define what the organization wants to be, long-range planning is forced to build a composite picture of the organization by projecting every detail of the business forward. How else can it arrive at a total view of the organization in the future? Such effort acts as a deterrent to change; it transforms most long-range plans into Gothic structures of inflexibility. This inflexibility makes it difficult to react to unanticipated changes in the environment and to adjust plans accordingly.* The modification of long-

* For an account of such inflexibility, see "Corporate Planning: Piercing Future Fog in the Executive Suite," *Business Week,* April 28, 1975, pp. 46–54.

range plans usually occurs only when events reach crisis proportions.

8. Long-range planning is really more short-range than anyone cares to admit. Long-range planning theory suggests that planning should project out five years and then recede back to the first year. But how can this be done in the absence of a structured framework for looking ahead five years? Lacking this, the sheer force of necessity leads managers to reverse the theory and begin by projecting from the first year. In addition, projections which are farther out are "iffy." Since there is so much work involved, the first year usually gets the most thorough analysis. After all, the manager knows he can make changes in following years; it is only the coming year that cannot be changed—this year becomes the budget. The shorter the time focus, the more easily a manager is locked into the constraints of current operations, and the less likely he is to be influenced by information of potential strategic significance. Anyway, most rewards for performance are only measured by first-year results.

CONCLUSION

Our own work has been conducted where strategy happens: with top managers in their organizations. From that vantage, we saw a critical need to separate strategic or directional thinking from long-range planning and operational thinking. The purpose of this chapter was to make that separation and to set the stage for an exploration of several other basic needs which must be understood before we can proceed to talk about improving strategic thinking.

CHAPTER TWO

Taking Stock of Your "Strategic I. Q."

Strategic anxiety is a many-sided syndrome. Some managers express this anxiety by noting that their organization is adrift, that it has no central purpose, that the top team is not "pulling together," that divisions are more like competitors than interdependent entities. Others intuitively sense where they are going, but complain that their colleagues or subordinates are not on the same frequency. How, they ask, can we get strategy out in the open? Still others complain that their organization's strategy is vague, poorly conceived or mere window dressing. In one company, conflict over corporate strategy between the chairman and president has sent chills down the spines of other top managers. Another company feels it must make a transition from a single-product, narrowly based market position. A new strategy must be set. The question is, how?

The common denominator of strategic anxiety is the presence of one or more strategic needs which have gone unfulfilled. While the organizations we have worked with vary as to industry and size, and are located in different countries, we have noticed that top executives are arrested by very similar concerns.

We have already examined the most critical strategic need that top managers must address: the separation of strategic thinking from long-range planning and operations. This chapter presents a series of snapshots of some of the other important needs we have observed in talking with key executives in corporate boardrooms and divisional headquarters. These include: *The need for focus.* Many statements of strategy are just too abstract to provide guidance to key decision makers. *The need for congruence.* There is a lack of a common way to tie together corporate, business unit and staff department directions. *The need to respond strategically to change.*

This chapter will discuss each of these needs and will provide you with an opportunity to test your "Strategic I.Q."

THE NEED FOR STRATEGIC FOCUS

When we say there is a need for strategic focus, we are not saying that managers have been lining up to tell us that they are all chronically suffering from a lack of focus. They don't have to. When you listen to what top executives are saying, when you examine their statements of strategy, you come away knowing that often the organization's strategy is vague, or that it lacks specificity, or that it is too complicated to serve as a framework to guide key decision makers.

Some strategies lack focus simply because they are too abstract.

Take, for example, this strategy statement from one of America's top companies. As the organization defines itself:

> Our business is the creation of machines and methods to help find solutions to the increasingly complex problems of business, government, science, space exploration, education, medicine, and nearly every other area of human endeavor.

What guidance does this statement give executives who must set strategies for their divisions, or who must make product or market choices for the next several years? What guidance does it provide for the allocation of resources and the determination of key results? Virtually none. The entire expanse of human activity is presumably legitimate ground for managers in this organization to pursue.

Some strategy statements lack focus because they are too massive.

"Kitchen-sink" strategies leave nothing to the imagination. They include so much detail about the organization that it is difficult to determine what is really important. Often this detail causes strategic and operational considerations to be mixed. Statements about the nature and direction of the business stand side by side with operational philosophy, goals and policies.

In one company, managers produced a strategy statement that ran six single-spaced pages. Consider some of the elements of this statement:

1. We will staff our organization with highly competent people capable of growth and compensate them well in relation to how they manage.

4. Our General Products and Plastics Division must remain the leading supplier of paper and plastic products to our markets in all aspects of quality and service.

6. Our operations should be judged on the basis of actual performance versus budget with periodic formal reviews.

7. We should continue to develop as a major packaging supplier with a broader range of products, placing high priority on internal development of food packaging, partitions, and other related products.

11. We must improve our financial reporting and product costing to provide more accurate and timely information for control and pricing.

13. We should expand export sales wherever practical and profitable, generally utilizing facilities of the International Division to perform this function.

19. In general, we will establish a new plant or introduce a new product line or product only if the return on investment is projected to exceed 20 percent before taxes within three years.

Statements of strategy that roll on and on without delineating priorities and without separating strategic and operational considerations are not helpful. The critical interrelationships among products, markets, capabilities and results are lost beneath the morass of operational philosophies and policies that relate to the day-to-day running of the business. As one executive put it, "You can't tell what's in the background and what should be up front. You can't focus attention; you can't grab hold of and use your strategy."

Review the statements listed above and ask yourself which of them are strategic; that is, they address the nature and direction of the organization, *what* it wants to be in the future. And ask which are operational; that is, they say something about *how* the organization will get there. Items 4, 7, 13 and 19 are more strategic. Items 1, 6 and 11 are more operational. Operational statements must be identified and separated so they will not confuse top management in its attempt to bring a strategic focus to the organization.

THE NEED FOR CONGRUENCE

For an organization to really "pull together" strategically, there must be congruence between the corporate strategy and the strategies of other units in the organization. "Congruence" does not mean that units in the organization are pre-empted from having their own strategy. The large modern organization is too complex, too diversified, to be a monolith. Strategic business units or product/market groups require their own strategies, but these strategies must complement one another and be supportive of the corporate strategy.

Staff groups are also headed somewhere. As with line units, staff groups have resources, products or services, markets or customers, at their command and results to achieve. They too can get caught up in their own plans and projections and veer off in a different direction from the rest of the organization. They too need a strategy which supports corporate and business-unit strategies and which guides their planning and decision making.

Without congruence, the organization's strategy, its plans and its allocation of resources will simply not be aligned and the odds of its achieving its most important results will be substantially lessened.

Many organizations do not have the connecting thread of strategy to keep their diversified activities integrated. Take a large commercial bank in the midwestern United States. It had what one vice president called a "decentralized, non-participative management style." In effect, the bank was a collection of semi-autonomous operating entities. There was very little linkage between such functions as trust, money management, commercial loans and retail banking. "Cross selling" became a buzz word, but there was little action to bring it about. There was also virtually no clear working relationship between the international and domestic sides of the business. Department heads worked directly with "someone at the top" and they tended to pursue their own goals. Once a year, the separate departments competed for the maximum they could get from corporate operating and capital budgets. Once supply was apportioned, each digested its slice in its own way.

These departments became protective of their "turf" when changes were proposed to better integrate the organization. According to the vice president quoted above, the departments had too long been pursuing separate strategies, ones which gave them "the seemingly wonderful advantage of being left alone." They simply would not be moved in the direction the president wanted, until an approach was developed to better define the bank's strategy and to redefine the strategies of each of the divisions and departments within the overall strategy.

The need for congruence is not only perceptible when departments are independent and antagonistic competitors for resources. It is also evident when management tells you that a division or a product group or a key staff function is simply not understood by the rest of the company. As organizations expand, they usually become more complex. Whatever the pattern of expansion—product/market proliferation, horizontal or vertical integration, the conglomerate route—business units may become different from one another in the direction they take and resources they require. When there is no common strategic bond, these differences become difficult to understand and, often, to tolerate. And when this happens, discussion of strategic matters at the corporate level and even among divisions tends to go underground. A division vice president of one organization recounts this example:

> In our end of the business, market share is critically important. It gives us an external measurement of what we have to be and do to compete. But I can remember when, in the corporate circuit, talking about market share was a dirty word. You simply didn't mention it. Frankly, this represented a kind of stupidity that existed because of a lack of knowledge of the interrelationships between the different functions of the business. And this kept us from discussing what was most vital to us and needed to be discussed elsewhere in the organization.

We have run up against much evidence of the lack of congruence within organizations. For example:

- In a large paper manufacturing company, managers in one division pursued a plant expansion policy that stood in opposition to a longer-term corporate marketing policy.

- A division of a diversified international organization acquired three auto-parts companies because of the compatibility of their products and capabilities. Division strategy called for the thorough integration of the three companies. Yet, operations of the three continued as though they were still independent. One of the companies, in fact, went to the open market to acquire subsystem components which could have been purchased internally.
- A large printing company acquired two book manufacturers who continued to bid against each other to outside book publishers.
- A wood-processing company had a strategy which dictated that it capture a significant segment of the wooden door market in Western Canada and the U.S. Unfortunately, the relevant division had different plans. It sought, instead, to diversify and made an extensive effort to penetrate the tubular furniture market.
- A large chemical company had two bosses. It was a division of a large subsidiary with headquarters outside the U.S. and yet it was tied to the worldwide bulk chemical group of the parent organization. The subsidiary was pushing the division to be a profitable producer and marketer of finished chemical products to its existing markets. The parent organization wanted it to supply raw materials to its worldwide network. The chemical division was in the middle of competing strategies.
- A specialty beverage company had a product-development department which spent considerable time and money developing a non-natural base product, using flavoring and alcohol. The product, if marketed, would have significantly compromised the integrity of the existing product line.

The examples are legion and the point is clear. When the strategies of business units are not in line with the corporate strategy or when they are not in line with one another, product, market and resource decisions can conflict. The allocation of resources *in advance* cannot be guided by the organization's strategy. It must be handled some other way. For example, some companies allocate resources as though they were the U.S. government. Like the government, corporate planning makes a resource decision based either on short-term expediency, or on who "hollers" the loudest. In other companies, the persuasive manager commands the scarcest resources. The real question is, how do you want *your* resources allocated: by your overall organization and business-unit strategies or some other way?

THE NEED FOR A STRATEGIC RESPONSE TO CHANGE

A newly appointed president of a consumer-goods company is facing a mess. He described it this way:

> The company started like many companies, as an entrepreneurial, free-wheeling affair. It sailed pretty close to the wind; there were a few nasty bumps in the first years, but the company kept growing. As it developed in the last three years, that style of management didn't work any longer. The company began to feel the cold wind of competition and a very hostile climate.
>
> This company had no explicitly stated strategy to guide its operational decision making. Changes were being made without a clear strategy. The company was driven by a "shoot-from-the-hip" Chairman of the Board who used intuition and "a gang of boys around the table" to make major decisions. The company decided to buy a new plant based on short-term, return-on-investment considerations. The plant was adequate in size, close to raw materials, efficiently equipped and in an area with favorable government regulations. Soon six additional plants were purchased in other locations. Long-term strategic objectives took second place to the whim and caprice of the moment. Financially, the company became dependent on short-term loans and the good will of the banks. To run these plants at capacity, the company went into a new and substantially different product line and it had to enter new markets domestically and internationally. That was a disaster. The new products did not move and, worse, they eroded the quality image of the existing, more expensive product line.

The incoming president knew that the company's attempts at restoring its dwindling market position and its plummeting profits were unguided by a larger sense of strategic direction. The changes that were made were erratic and very costly. As the company's prospects continued to deteriorate, top managers became increasingly frustrated and pessimistic. "When I came aboard," the president reported, "the people here thought our problems were virtually unsolvable or required someone with a massively developed instinct. People thought I was the guy with the magic wand."

But the president was not a magician and more than a magic wand was needed. The company needed a strategy to guide the top management team as it made the necessary changes. Without a clear strategy these managers had nothing except operational criteria against which to test their judgments.

Every change, the Chinese proverb says, brings an opportunity —and a threat, Murphy would add. All organizations are confronted by change. How well an organization can negotiate the hurdles of change is key to its survival and success. Some change is external. It occurs "outside" the organization—in the environment—and is beyond the organization's immediate control. For example, technological, economic and socio-political trends and events; changes in forms of competition and direct competitors; changes in customer or supplier priorities and preferences. Even though external, these types of changes can have a profound impact on the organization.

Other change is internal. For example, changes in product/market proliferation, organizational structure, capital requirements, personnel, business philosophy and management style. These occur "inside" an organization and are directly within its sphere of decision-making capability.

In spite of the differences between external and internal change, there is one important similarity: both require raising strategic questions first, before any action is taken. A response to external change should begin with the questions: What does our strategy suggest about how we should react to this change? Does it suggest a reformulation, a modification or an extension of our current strategy? Does it suggest that we maintain the strategic *status quo?* Knee-jerk operational reactions to the oil cartel, environmental pressures, consumerism and increasing government intervention suggest that some organizations have not carefully considered strategic responses to these kinds of changes. And, such changes will become increasingly significant in the future.

Take a company in the industrial manufacturing and supply business. Its primary product is a holding device for customers in the heavy equipment and transportation industries. The company is well-run, has an enviable balance sheet and a predominant market share. Yet, the Chief Executive Officer is losing sleep. What is on his mind is not his competition but his customers. The holding device he manufactures is currently vital to his customers. An indispensable product sold to a cornered market sounds great, but this CEO's utopia could be short-lived. His customers are working to eliminate the need for the device. Five years from now both the product and his organization may well become obsolete.

"Where should I take the business beyond the next five years?" asks the CEO. "What new products and markets should we have on tap when the moment of truth arrives?" "What can I build on?" The questions on this CEO's mind are the most basic strategic questions. After raising them, this CEO stepped back to examine the nature and direction of his business in light of the changing environment. Once he decided what the new longer-range strategy should be, he could make operational decisions accordingly.

A response to a proposed internal change should begin with the questions: Is this change in support of our strategy? Does it suggest a reformulation, a modification or an extension of our current strategy? Is the proposed change worth it? Once a proposed internal change passes these questions, the discussion can move to operational matters.

The founder of a highly successful money-management organization was a shrewd financial analyst and a no-nonsense, one-man-rule proponent. The strategy of the organization, to the extent there was one, resided in the founder's head. The only "strategic" question even uttered by his top managers was "What does the boss think?"

Unfortunately, the founder met an untimely death, leaving a group of talented but undirected principals to run the business. One thing was clear to these managers. They now had the autonomy to make operating decisions. However, as one of the principals of the company recalls, "There was also the widespread feeling that we needed criteria to explain why, say, a new product idea was good or bad. While we needed more autonomy in our respective areas, we also needed a corporate framework for the individual decisions we would now be making. We needed a lot more objective and penetrating questions about where we were going."

The really important change, it turned out, was a change in management style. Key decision-making responsibility would now be shared among the top managers of the business. These managers were anxious to get on with the task of making operational decisions, but they were smart enough to realize that such decisions had to be guided by a strategic framework.

The executives in each of the above examples clearly saw the strategic dimensions of the task before them. They saw that strategy not only guides change; it gives change definition. "With a strategy," a CEO told us, "we at least know what our starting point is. When a change has to be made, we have a place to begin." This, in a nutshell, is the meaning of a strategic response to change. It is using your strategy as a "place to start" when you assess the impact of an external change or when you contemplate making an internal change. A strategic response to change requires a strategy.

WHAT IS YOUR "STRATEGIC I.Q."?

If you are concerned about possible confusion between strategy and planning in your organization, or lack of strategic focus, congruence or response to change, you may be in strategic trouble. To test your organization's "Strategic I.Q.," ask yourself:

- Has your top management consciously determined what it wants the organization to be—the nature and direction of the business—over the next few years?
- Do you know the specifics of your organization's strategy?
- Would each of the other key managers share the same vision of your organization's future strategic direction?
- Is your strategy sufficiently clear so you and the key managers around you can readily agree upon what new products and markets your current strategy would include *and* exclude?
- Is your statement of strategy used for making future product and market choices? (As opposed to making such choices solely on the basis of cost/return analysis, manpower availability, skills required, and the like.)
- Are your strategic deliberations held separately from your long-range planning efforts?
- Is your future strategy clearly determining what you plan,

project and budget? (As opposed to your plans, projections and budgets determining your strategy.)

- Are the assumptions you generate about the environment used for setting strategy? (As opposed to their being used mainly as a basis for long-range planning projections.)
- Is your future strategy clearly determining your decisions relating to acquisitions, capital appropriations and new systems? (As opposed to such decisions really determining your strategy.)
- Do your line divisions or business units have clear, stated strategies?
- Do these line-division or business-unit strategies fully support your corporate strategy?
- Do your key staff departments have clear, stated strategies?
- Do these staff-department strategies fully support corporate and business-unit strategies?
- Is the overall performance of your organization and its business units reviewed on both strategic accomplishment and operating results?

The more of these questions to which you answered "no," or could not firmly answer "yes," the more your company's strategy is in trouble. If you answered all "no," then you can probably hold last rites for strategy in your organization. It is officially deceased. Whatever your "Strategic I.Q." the rest of this book is designed to help you improve that score.

CONCLUSION

Chapter One covered the first and critically important theme we observed from our work with top management on strategy formulation: the need to separate strategic thinking from long-range planning and operations. Chapter Two expanded that theme to show the need to improve the quality of strategic thinking. A second equally important theme is the need for an approach: a central or unifying concept to guide strategy setting at the highest corporate and divisional levels. We call that concept the Driving Force. It is the subject of Chapter Three.

Driving Force and the Nine Basic Strategic Areas

THE NEED FOR A STRATEGIC FRAMEWORK

We have defined strategy as a framework to guide those choices that determine the nature and direction of an organization. But what are those "choices" and what constitutes a framework within which those choices can be made?

Major directional choices confront an organization almost every day. They include choices about the kinds of products the organization will and will not consider, the geographic markets and market segments or customer groups it will and will not serve, the key capabilities or resources necessary to support those products and markets, the growth and return required, and the allocation of resources.

How these choices are made determines the nature and direction of your organization. If they are made within the context of a strategic framework, your organization's direction is clearly under the control of the top managers who develop that framework. If these choices are made in the absence of a strategic framework, you abdicate that control and run the risk of having a direction which is fragmented and in the hands of whoever is making these choices.

For a strategy to be practical and useful, it must be a framework which specifies the scope and boundaries for each of these areas of choice. Further, it must show how each is related to the other. The single most important question becomes: How can that framework be built?

To answer this question, a clear and simple concept to guide top management is needed—a central "hook" which can serve as a basis to develop a Strategic Framework. We call that concept the Driving Force.

THE DRIVING FORCE

It might be said without much oversimplification that an organization is the sum total of the products it offers and the geographic markets and market segments or customer groups it serves. Indeed, much of an organization's resources and capabilities, its plans and structure, its decision making and problem solving—in short, all of its important activities—are ultimately directed toward its products and markets. Thus, the most fundamental strategic decision is: What should the scope of our products and markets be?

This is a tough question. As a key manager, you undoubtedly have had to face new product, market expansion, or acquisition decisions. When considering such decisions, what led you and other key managers to a "go" or "no go" conclusion? Here, we are not raising questions about a specific factor, event or criterion that may have guided the decision—for example, pressure from the competition, a new government regulation, presumed growth or profitability, or a resource scarcity.

Rather, we are asking questions about the nature and direction of the business. For example, Why are you in the business you are in and not another? Why are you making the products you are making and not others? Why are you in the markets you are in and not others? The Driving Force concept is the key to strategically managing major product and market choices that your organization must resolve. Thus, we define Driving Force as *the primary determiner of the scope of future products and markets*. The Driving Force and the product and market scope it suggests provide the basis for defining the other choices in the strategic profile. Thus:

STRATEGIC FRAMEWORK

DRIVING FORCE

- Future Product Scope
- Future Market Scope:
  Geographic and Segment

- Key Cabilities Required
  to Support the Driving
  Force
- Size/Growth Guidelines
- Return/Profit Guidelines
- Business Unit Mission
  Statements to Guide
  Resource Allocation

The Driving Force and Strategic Framework must be developed within a specific future time frame. The following criteria help to establish that time frame:

- Lead time for product development
- Market trend
- Rate of change in customer needs and preferences
- Rate of technological change
- Capital intensity—degree of flexibility
- Rate of social, political, economic change
- Product life-cycle

More than a few managers are unaware of their organization's Driving Force. They are somewhat like the inhabitants of a cave that the philosopher Plato once described. These inhabitants spent their entire lives, from birth to old age, puzzling over the eerie figures that moved along the cave walls and then mysteriously disappeared. The inhabitants knew everything about these figures. They knew their size and shape, and knew precisely when they came and left. But one fact they did not know: a distant hole in the roof of the cave had let in sunlight. The inhabitants were looking at shadows!

Obviously, top managers are much more sophisticated. But, without probing beyond the most visible features of their organization —the array of products and markets—they, too, have an incomplete understanding of their reality. For them, the organization's Driving Force remains something of a mystery.

Without an explicit understanding of the Driving Force, guidance for your organization's future product and market choices will mainly come from two sources. First, by reviewing past product and market decisions, some sort of logic can be devised and applied to future product and market decisions. Second, you can make future product and market decisions based on operational criteria. The sum total of those decisions becomes your strategy. These can hardly be effective ways to set strategy. Strategy setting is either an exercise which involves the top team in consciously determining the Driving Force, and then using it to determine and define the organization's Product and Market Scope, or it is an exercise in futility. How, indeed, can the future scope of products and markets be clearly delineated when the Driving Force determining that scope remains unarticulated in the thinking of top managers? Worse yet, how can the future Product and Market Scope be delineated when there is unarticulated and unresolved disagreement about what should be driving the future of the organization?

Without the concept of Driving Force and the Strategic Framework it produces, many executives have become frustrated with their attempts to set strategy. The scene is all too familiar. Top management leaves its operational concerns behind and takes off for the mountaintop to do some hard strategic thinking. What happens? The strategy-setting experience tends to fall apart. The CEO has a way to proceed, but so does everyone else. Information about the company and the environment is collected, but there are conflicting opinions on how to use it. Strategic and operational considerations get garbled. This makes it easy to veer off into more comfortable operational issues. Thoughtful differences about possible future directions are difficult to resolve. Real commitment comes only at very general levels. So it goes.

Once you have determined your organization's Driving Force, you have set its underlying momentum, the key to its nature and direction. And, once you understand the significance of the Driving Force, it becomes the basis for setting each dimension of the Strategic Framework. Ultimately, the Driving Force gives top managers a central idea or concept in terms of which they can both see the future of their organization and assess the product and market decisions that will—or will not—get them there.

The rest of this chapter examines the concept of Driving Force. The next chapter will discuss how that Driving Force is used to develop the other dimensions of the Strategic Framework.

DRIVING FORCE: WHERE DOES IT COME FROM?

Our research suggests that there are nine basic Strategic Areas, all of which can decisively affect and influence the nature and direction of any organization. These nine Strategic Areas can be grouped into three categories:

Category	*Strategic Area*
PRODUCTS/MARKETS	PRODUCTS OFFERED
	MARKET NEEDS
CAPABILITIES	TECHNOLOGY
	PRODUCTION CAPABILITY
	METHOD OF SALE
	METHOD OF DISTRIBUTION
	NATURAL RESOURCES
RESULTS	SIZE/GROWTH
	RETURN/PROFIT

All nine Areas are critically important to every company. However, in every one of the organizations with which we have worked, we have found that *one and only one* of the above nine Areas should be the Driving Force for the total organization. Likewise, for any business unit within that organization there should be only one Driving Force, though not necessarily the same as the Driving Force of the total organization. This is not to say that one or two of these key Strategic Areas might not be very close to the Driving Force as secondary screens for product and market choices. But, the ultimate question is: When the final decision about a product or a market is made, which of these Strategic Areas proved to be most decisive? This is the Driving Force.

Surprising as it might seem, in a number of organizations there is initial disagreement about even the current Driving Force. In some cases there are actually several Driving Forces in the minds of the various executives, pulling the organization in different directions as major product, market, and resource decisions are made. Once top management understands the concept of Driving Force, it can use that understanding to reach agreement on which Strategic Area represents the organization's current Driving Force. With a clearly stated current Driving Force, top management has a consistent starting point for considering future strategic options.

When we say that one of the Strategic Areas serves as the Driving Force, we do not mean to imply that there is only one right Driving Force for an organization and all other possibilities are wrong. Determining a future Driving Force is not a matter of making a moral judgment but of making a tough, practical choice, given such factors as an organization's strengths and vulnerabilities, its competitive position, its basic beliefs and the external/environmental events that are likely to exert an impact on the organization. For any organization, the best future Driving Force evolves from the rigors of testing possible future Driving Forces against these factors. This tough critique narrows the field to the one Driving Force which takes greatest advantage of that organization's internal and external opportunities and strengths and overcomes threats and vulnerabilities.

Nor are we saying that the Driving Force and the process of arriving at it eliminates the judgment, the "gut feel" of top management about the organization's strategic direction. Understanding and applying the concept of Driving Force is the best way to make that judgment visible. Once visible, the Driving Force helps to shape and refine that judgment so it can be consciously used to guide future product and market choices.

Given the importance of the nine Strategic Areas, we have devoted considerable time to defining, testing and validating each

Area. The following descriptions of each Strategic Area are the results of these efforts. In order to protect confidentiality, the examples we use to illustrate each Strategic Area as a Driving Force are not taken from our strategy clients. Instead, they are taken from observing the product and market actions of well-known organizations in a number of industries. Your experience and knowledge of these organizations may lead you to another conclusion about their Driving Force. This is fine. The purpose of our examples is to help illustrate the concept of Driving Force. The only sure-fire way to know an organization's Driving Force is to know the thinking of top management that led to specific product and market actions.

1. PRODUCTS OFFERED

Definition

Products are whatever an organization offers to the markets it serves, including ongoing support and maintenance. A product may be defined individually *or* as a line or grouping of products or sub-products. Products are defined on the basis of common characteristics such as functions performed, customer needs satisfied, size or form, durability, etc.

PRODUCTS OFFERED *As the Driving Force*

The organization with PRODUCTS OFFERED as its Driving Force has a concept of its products which is key to the future markets it serves and to the ways in which it will meet the needs of those markets. The PRODUCTS OFFERED-driven organization will continue to produce and deliver products similar to those it has. New products will have characteristics very similar to those of current products. This organization will focus on higher penetration of its current geographic markets and the particular market segments or customer groups it serves. This organization will seek new geographic markets and market segments where there is a need for its products. It will constantly be looking for ways to improve or extend these products. Its capabilities will be directed toward supporting the effective development, production, promotion, sale, delivery and servicing of these products or services. When an organization is driven by PROD-

UCTS OFFERED, it does not necessarily lack marketing skill. In fact, some of the best marketing capabilities may be found in organizations driven by PRODUCTS OFFERED.

Selected Examples

The actions of the following organizations would suggest that their Driving Force is PRODUCTS OFFERED:

> Ford Motor Company
> Metro-Goldwyn-Mayer, Inc.
> Bank of America

2. MARKET NEEDS

Definition

A market is a group of current or potential buyers or end users who share common needs. Market groupings could be formed on the basis of age, income, sex, education, ethnic background, occupation, industry, etc. These groupings may be formed or limited geographically.

MARKET NEEDS *As the Driving Force*

The organization whose Driving Force is MARKET NEEDS will provide a range of products to fill current and emerging needs in the market segments or customer groups it serves. It will be constantly looking for alternative ways to fill the needs it is currently filling. It will also be constantly searching for new or emerging needs in the market segments it serves. The MARKET NEEDS-driven organization develops or acquires new and different products to meet needs in its market segments. When it explores new geographical markets or market segments, they will have characteristics similar to those it currently serves. For the organization driven by MARKET NEEDS, significant resources will be directed to functions such as needs analysis and market research. The timely development and offering of new products is very critical. Do not confuse the Strategic Area

MARKET NEEDS with the typical functions of marketing. Because an organization places emphasis on marketing functions such as advertising, promotion and market research, it does *not* necessarily follow that it is MARKET NEEDS-driven. Marketing is important to any company, regardless of Driving Force. However, only in some companies do the needs of the market determine the products.

Selected Examples

The actions of the following organizations would suggest that their Driving Force is MARKET NEEDS:

> Playboy Enterprises, Inc.
> Gillette Company
> U.S. Department of Health and Human Services
> Merrill Lynch & Co. Inc.

3. TECHNOLOGY

Definition

A technology is a learned body of knowledge which is reproducible and subject to frequent update and extension. This would include the skills and knowledge possessed by those within the discipline, science or profession involved. It also includes the necessary systems, equipment and support facilities such as laboratories, libraries, and the like.

TECHNOLOGY As the Driving Force

An organization that is driven by TECHNOLOGY offers *only* products or services that emanate from or capitalize on its technological capability. In such an organization, technology determines the scope of products offered and markets served, rather than the products and markets determining the technology. The TECHNOLOGY-driven organization would seek a variety of applications for its technology. It would do this through the products or services it develops from this technology, or by selling the output of its technology to those who would develop further products or services. While the

TECHNOLOGY-driven organization usually strives to be the technological and innovative leader in its field, it will not always be the initiator of technological breakthroughs. Many TECHNOLOGY-driven organizations focus on converting breakthroughs made elsewhere to a variety of applications.

Selected Examples

The actions of the following organizations would suggest that their Driving Force is TECHNOLOGY:

> E. I. du Pont de Nemours & Company
> U.S. Center for Disease Control
> Texas Instruments

4. PRODUCTION CAPABILITY

Definition

Production capability includes the production know-how, processes, systems and equipment required to make specific products, and the capability to improve those processes. In a service organization, the production capability includes those processes and skills required to provide the service(s) and any necessary support materials, procedures, programs, etc.

PRODUCTION CAPABILITY As the Driving Force

An organization that is driven by PRODUCTION CAPABILITY offers *only* those products that can be made or developed using its production know-how, processes, systems, and equipment.

There are two very different forms of PRODUCTION CAPABILITY as a Driving Force. First, consider the commodity type of business. This organization will manufacture products with long runs and economies of scale. Focus will be on efficiency in production with emphasis on those products with maximum efficiency. New products could be quite different from current products, while still utilizing existing production know-how, processes, systems and equipment.

This organization may make products for another organization as a means of utilizing this capability. It may also lease or sell its capability to others.

A second form of PRODUCTION CAPABILITY, as a Driving Force, is the job-shop type of business. This organization produces a wide range of products, sub-products or parts which utilize its production know-how, processes, systems, and equipment. New products or work accepted would utilize these same production capabilities. Over time this job shop would probably add supportive equipment in small increments to broaden its base and provide additional flexibility and value added.

Selected Examples

The actions of the following organizations would suggest that their Driving Force is PRODUCTION CAPABILITY:

> United States Steel Corporation
> The Service Bureau Corporation
> R. R. Donnelly & Sons Company
> International Paper Company

5. METHOD OF SALE

Definition

The method of sale is the *primary* way an organization convinces current or potential customers or users to buy its products. This method of sale may be directed to both its customer and the end user if different from its customer. This primary method of sale may be supported in a number of ways, such as advertising, display, direct mail, etc.

METHOD OF SALE *As the Driving Force*

An organization that is driven by its METHOD OF SALE will determine the products it provides, the markets it enters, and its geographic scope on the basis of the capabilities and limitations of that primary METHOD OF SALE. An organization that is driven by METHOD OF

SALE may seek other sales approaches that are similar to or compatible with its current METHOD OF SALE. Its other capabilities, particularly method of distribution, will be developed to support its METHOD OF SALE. This organization may sell products from other organizations to gain maximum advantage from its METHOD OF SALE Driving Force.

Selected Examples

The actions of the following organizations would suggest that their Driving Force is METHOD OF SALE:

Avon Products, Inc.
Book-of-the-Month Club, Inc.
The Franklin Mint Corporation
Spiegel, Inc. (retail catalogue sales)

6. METHOD OF DISTRIBUTION

Definition

The method of distribution is the way products reach the customer, including field or in-route storage. This includes significant know-how, systems and equipment to support the method of distribution. This *does not* include how the potential customer is persuaded to buy the product. For example, a rack display would be part of the method of sale. The method of distribution may be directed to both the customer and the end user if different from the customer.

METHOD OF DISTRIBUTION *As the Driving Force*

An organization that is driven by METHOD OF DISTRIBUTION will determine the products it sells, the customers it sells them to, and its geographic scope on the basis of those kinds of products or services and customers that can be handled through its established distribution channels. It may seek other distribution channels that are similar to its current METHOD OF DISTRIBUTION. Its other capabilities, particularly method of sale, will be developed to support that METHOD OF DISTRIBUTION. This organization may distribute products from other organizations to gain maximum advantage from its distribution network.

Selected Examples

The actions of the following organizations would suggest that their Driving Force is METHOD OF DISTRIBUTION:

> American Telephone and Telegraph Corporation
> McDonald's Corporation
> Canteen Service Company

7. NATURAL RESOURCES

Definition

Natural Resources are those actual and potential forms of wealth supplied by nature. These would include coal, oil, metals, wood, water, usable land, etc. They would not include human resources or resources produced by man, such as money, processed foodstuffs, etc.

NATURAL RESOURCES As the Driving Force

An organization with NATURAL RESOURCES as a Driving Force would develop its products and markets through the use or conservation of its NATURAL RESOURCES. It would concentrate on control of those resources as a means of increasing their value. An organization that is NATURAL RESOURCE-driven may sell those NATURAL RESOURCES to others or turn them into products. Just because an organization owns or buys natural resources to support its products, such as a steel company, does not mean that its Driving Force is NATURAL RESOURCES.

Selected Examples

The actions of the following organizations would suggest that their Driving Force is NATURAL RESOURCES:

Gulf Oil Corporation
The Province of Alberta, Canada
De Beers Consolidated Mines
The U.S. Forest Service

8. SIZE/GROWTH

Definition

The Size/Growth of an organization is defined as its overall size and/ or rate of growth as measured by the most appropriate indexes. For some organizations, size is most important and rate of growth is how it gets there. For other organizations, rate of growth is most important and size is only the result.

SIZE/GROWTH *As the Driving Force*

An organization whose Driving Force is SIZE/GROWTH determines the scope of the products it offers, the markets it serves, and its geographic scope from its desire to become larger or smaller. SIZE/ GROWTH is the Driving Force *only* if the desire to grow leads to a change in the product and market scope. An organization that wants rapid growth, but within its current product and market scope, *is not* SIZE/GROWTH-driven. The organization with SIZE/GROWTH as its Driving Force will set levels of size and growth significantly different from its current level of performance. This organization will push into new unrelated products or markets. SIZE/GROWTH does not automatically mean getting larger. It may mean a controlled reduction if such a reduction determines the scope of products and markets. SIZE/GROWTH is not likely to be a long-term Driving Force. Organizations typically remain SIZE/GROWTH-driven for a limited period of time to enable them to move toward another Driving Force.

Selected Examples

The actions of the following organizations would suggest that their Driving Force is SIZE/GROWTH:

The Continental Group, Inc.
Shearson, Loeb, Rhoades, Inc.

Since SIZE/GROWTH is always an interim Driving Force, it can best be seen at a particular time in an organization's life. For example:

The City University of New York (1960s)
Boise Cascade Corporation (1960s)
Litton Industries, Inc. (late 1950s, 1960s)

9. RETURN/PROFIT

Definition

Return/Profit is the financial result of an organization's effort. This result may be measured in a variety of ways, such as a percent of sales, return on assets or return on equity. In non-profit organizations, measures of return may be in terms of cost/benefit ratio, budgetary control, or in quality or degree of services rendered.

RETURN/PROFIT *As the Driving Force*

An organization that is RETURN/PROFIT-driven will determine the scope of its products and markets from its desire for specific levels of return/profit. RETURN/PROFIT is the Driving Force *only* if a change is made in the Product or Market Scope in order to achieve its RETURN/PROFIT requirements. An organization that wants to increase its return and profit and yet stay within its current Product Scope and Market Scope is *not* RETURN/PROFIT-driven. To be RETURN/PROFIT-driven these return and profit targets must be used to determine the scope of future products or markets and *not* as a screen for particular products or markets to select within that Product Scope. This Driving Force may lead an organization to seek a variety of unrelated products over time, or it may lead an organization to change from one line of related products to a different line of related products because of RETURN/PROFIT considerations. The RETURN/PROFIT-driven organization's product/market choices may be constrained or limited by its need to produce a consistent return.

Selected Examples

The actions of the following organizations would suggest that their Driving Force is RETURN/PROFIT.

International Telephone and Telegraph Corporation
Gulf and Western Industries, Inc.
R. J. Reynolds Industries, Inc.

THE DRIVING FORCE: IT MAKES A DIFFERENCE

Your organization's Product and Market Scope, the kinds of capabilities required to support that Product and Market Scope, and its results in terms of Growth and Return, depend on its Driving Force. As a Driving Force, each of the nine Strategic Areas has a profoundly different impact on an organization. Thus, depending on the Driving Force you set, the kinds of products you offer and markets you serve will be quite different over time.

In fact, if you were the proverbial fly on the wall in a top executive's office in a MARKET NEEDS-driven company, the conversation about major product choices would be far different from what you would hear in a PRODUCTS OFFERED-driven or a RETURN/PROFIT-driven organization. With a MARKET NEEDS Driving Force, product discussion would focus more on such questions as: "Given our success with this product, what new approaches to filling that need is R & D working on?" "What other needs do our customers have?" "What new products should we develop to fill those needs?"

With a PRODUCTS OFFERED Driving Force, product discussion would be pitched to such questions as: "What is engineering doing with the results of that market research to improve next year's model?" "What are we doing to fill that gap in our current product line?" "This new product idea sounds great, but how does it support our present product concept?"

And, in a RETURN/PROFIT-driven organization, product discussion would revolve around such questions as: "I don't care about product or market synergy, will this new venture meet our profit targets?" "If we're going to achieve our profit objectives over the next few years, the question is: What's the best way to get into high profit businesses that are unrelated to what we are currently doing?''

DRIVING FORCE: TOOL FOR STRATEGY FORMULATION

Identifying your current Driving Force and then considering whether or not that Driving Force should be changed for the future is the most difficult aspect of strategy setting. Stakes are high. Assumptions about an uncertain future must be made, and values must be explicitly stated. Much soul-searching and a willingness to take a stand are required. Yet, your organization simply cannot be all things to all people.

Some executives have found that grappling with the Driving Force may also require a willingness to acknowledge—and acknowledge to subordinates, in the case of CEOs—that they were unclear in their understanding of the nature of their organization. One company president who recently joined the organization he now heads, recalled his mistaken notion of the company's Driving Force:

> I had a totally wrong view of what our Driving Force was. Given the expansion and acquisition program of the organization over the last few years, I thought our Driving Force was SIZE/GROWTH. We put a whole lot of money—at great risk—into buying various plants and companies. But in actual fact, when we took a hard look at our Driving Force, SIZE/GROWTH was not it. What linked these decisions together was TECHNOLOGY. That was our Driving Force. Our business was putting only those products on the market that stem from our extensive R & D effort.

Getting the top team to agree on a statement of strategy is not terribly difficult when discussion is unstructured and remains at a high level of abstraction. Few could argue with the following excerpt from one organization's statement of strategy:

> The primary goal of our organization is to achieve a higher level of profitability by supplying quality products to customers in a manner that takes into account both commercial interests and the broader needs of society. . . .

On the other hand, how helpful is the above statement in resolving future product and market choices? The concept of Driving Force and the process used to arrive at it keep honestly differing points of view from being camouflaged by the fuzz of abstraction. When discussion is sharply defined, the strategy statement which emerges is clear, specific and useful.

Compare the strategy statement above with its reformulated version below. The excerpts that follow are taken from the organization's description of its Driving Force:

> We are a PRODUCTS OFFERED company whose primary thrust is the manufacture and sale of specialized electronic components. Our focus will be on improving and extending our present products to better serve existing geographical markets.
>
> While we will concentrate our efforts in the specialized electronics components markets we serve in the United States, we will actively develop new international markets for our basic products. Canada, Mexico and Western Europe will be our initial targets.
>
> We will not dilute our available resources by doing research which diverts us from our present product lines. . . .

Without knowing anything more about this organization's strategy, which statement serves as a clearer, more specific guide for major product and market decisions? For example, assume you had to make a decision on a new product, an acquisition, a market expansion, or on allocation of resources for R & D. Which statement would be more instructive?

As a strategy-setting tool, the Driving Force is an instrument for bringing out different points of view about the future direction of the business. It is the mechanism for fleshing out those points of view, for resolving differences, and for formulating a specific statement of strategy. When you raise the questions—What, in the final analysis, has been determining our organization's Product/Market Scope? and, What should be?—there is simply nowhere to hide. You are forced to take a stand and to support that stand by a rigorous analysis of the available information.

To answer the first question—What is our current Driving Force? —you must analyze past product and market actions before you can come to a conclusion. For example, What determined our decision to accept or reject this new product, or to take advantage of, or stay away from, that new market opportunity? Why was an acquisition made or rejected?

It may be there is no single current Driving Force to which top management is committed; that, in reality, assumptions about different presumed Driving Forces conditioned various product, market and resource choices. This confusion really points to the need for a clear and committed future Driving Force and Strategic Framework within which product and market decisions can be made. On the other hand, there may be a clear and common understanding of current Driving Force. This provides a sound point of departure for exploring a future Driving Force and Strategic Framework.

Answering the second question—What should our future Driving Force be?—requires that you and the other top managers take a stand on the organization's future direction. It also requires the top team to do some hard thinking about the consequences of each Driving Force that surfaces as a future possibility. For example, how does each possible future Driving Force test against such factors as the organization's basic beliefs or unique strengths, critical environmental threats and opportunities, likely competitive actions, and growth and return expectations? What are the implications of each possible future Driving Force on current product or service and market priorities, and on likely new product and market choices? What would be the impact of each possible future Driving Force on the current Key Capabilities, SIZE/GROWTH and RETURN/PROFIT guidelines?

The process of gathering, analyzing and testing information in terms of the Driving Force enables top managers to make explicit what lies implicit in their past product and market choices, and what may be implicit in their thinking about the future direction of the organization. The concept of the Driving Force allows managers to develop and evaluate alternative future strategies for the organization. It also provides a mechanism for surfacing the differences in directional thinking among top managers and then reconciling those differences without compromising the clarity and usefulness of the final statement of strategy.

CHAPTER FOUR

The Power of the Driving Force

The impact of the Driving Force is substantial. It shapes each area of choice in the Strategic Framework and it is the unifying concept of an organization's strategy. Let us take a look at the relationship between the Driving Force and the other dimensions of the Strategic Framework: Future Product Scope, Future Market Scope, Key Capabilities Required, Size/Growth Guidelines, Return/Profit Guidelines and Business Unit Mission Statements.

Future Product Scope and Future Market Scope: We define "scope" as a set of common characteristics which describe the extent or boundary within which future product, geographic market, and market segment choices are made. These characteristics serve as a standard by which to test future product and market decisions. When these characteristics are clearly defined, managers can separate specific product and market choices which fall outside the organization's strategy from those that fall within it.

An organization's Driving Force is the basis for defining its Future Product and Market Scope. For example, one company had an entrepreneurial start with a breakthrough in chemistry applied to various tests in the health care field. It grew rapidly and expanded in all directions. Top management met and determined that its Driving Force was and should be TECHNOLOGY. The description of that Driving Force led to a tight set of product and market characteristics

58

which provided much better guidance and control for future product and market choices. Product characteristics included:

- Products shall meet a clinical and/or technical need for improvements in the present state of the art. Indirectly, this means we shall not use our resources to develop "me-too" products.
- Products shall constitute complete, self-contained, self-explanatory units.
- Products shall be based on biological substances or microorganisms and be intended for diagnosis or treatment monitoring in the health care field.
- Products will remain within the area of polymer chemistry.

Given the TECHNOLOGY Driving Force, several key market characteristics required redefinition. Geographic markets would now be concentrated worldwide where significant health care insurance was available. Customer group characteristics were broadened from a concentration on laboratories to include physicians and clinics.

Another example of the impact of the Driving Force on the Future Product and Market Scope involves a company that provided various products to the electrical energy field. It developed a PRODUCTION CAPABILITY Driving Force and redefined and broadened its product characteristics to reflect that Driving Force. These product characteristics included:

- Industrial products
- Electrical, mechanical, metallurgical properties
- High quality/reliability requirements
- After-sale service requirements
- Compatible with high technology inputs
- Low content of ferrous metals

In addition, several of the organization's market characteristics significantly changed. It shifted its focus to industries with a few large customers. It also sought specific customers who could not supply their own after-sale service and who required a system versus just a single product. Geographically, it would no longer cover the entire country, but would concentrate on major industrial areas.

Another company with a limited product line in the model toy-kit business shifted from a PRODUCTS OFFERED to a MARKET NEEDS Driving Force. This new Driving Force required it to segment its market much more carefully and identify the common characteristics of its major customer group. This enabled the company to seek a broader range of needs to fill for that customer group. These customer group characteristics included:

- Males
- Six to sixteen (primarily)
- Seventeen to twenty-one (secondarily)
- Average academic inclination
- Lower to middle income
- Maximum leisure time available
- Mechanically inclined
- High creative desires

Several of its product characteristics also required modification. Raw materials, formerly plastic, now included wood, metal and paper. Formerly, assembly required minimum skill. This was broadened to include varying levels of skill. Products, formerly of a military orientation, were diversified to include all authentic miniature reproductions of real-life items.

With tightly defined characteristics for Product Scope and Market Scope, top management can focus on developing or acquiring those products and developing those markets that fit within the intent and limits of the organization's Driving Force. This keeps management's time and energy, and the organization's capital, from being siphoned off in the pursuit of always exciting but really irrelevant opportunities.

Key Capabilities Required to Support the Driving Force: Every organization has capabilities which support its product and market choices. These capabilities include:

- Technology/Methodology
- Production
- Marketing
- Sales

- Distribution
- Raw Materials
- Financing
- Information Processing
- Human Resources
  —General Management
  —Functional Management

A certain level of quantity and proficiency in each of these Capabilities is required before any organization can function effectively. The Driving Force and the Future Product and Market Scope give priority to these Capabilities and determine precisely how each one will support the Driving Force. Given a particular Driving Force, Product Scope and Market Scope, some of these Capabilities will require a much higher level of quantity or proficiency than others. For example, if your future Driving Force is different from your current Driving Force or if your future Driving Force is a significant modification of your current Driving Force, certain of these Capabilities may require major change to support that new Driving Force and resulting Product and Market Scope. Capabilities that have been critical in the past may diminish in importance. Others may require significant changes in scope, limit or level of proficiency to support that future Driving Force.

A company we know was founded on the strength of a technological breakthrough. Its initial products were quite unique. While this company enjoyed a strong market position, its unique advantage was rapidly evaporating. Larger competitors were planning to muscle into the lucrative market this organization had built. In addition, proprietary technological breakthroughs became increasingly tough to make. In sizing up the situation, the top team opted to change the organization's Driving Force from TECHNOLOGY to PRODUCTS OFFERED.

Given the new PRODUCTS OFFERED thrust, TECHNOLOGY became a Key Capability but with a very different focus than it previously had as the Driving Force. The bulk of the organization's technological strength would now be directed toward making product improvements in its current product line. Frontier technological research would be replaced by efforts to keep these products up-to-date and in the forefront. In addition, given the new PRODUCTS

OFFERED Driving Force, Production and Sales became critically important Key Capabilities, as the company searched to keep its main products ahead of the well-heeled competition.

As a hedge against the much longer-term future, a very small but select part of the technology group was pulled out and given a budget and a mission to continue to explore leading-edge technology. This TECHNOLOGY-driven group was clearly separated from the PRODUCTS OFFERED strategy and was managed accordingly.

Another company had a narrow line of consumer products and a PRODUCTS OFFERED Driving Force. Its Key Capabilities were Production and Distribution. Given significant competitive pressure, the company attempted to capitalize on its strong franchise in the marketplace and began to move carefully toward a MARKET NEEDS Driving Force. Two Key Capabilities that had previously been of secondary importance now became very critical to support the new Driving Force. Acquiring and developing Marketing capability in all of its dimensions was essential. In addition, with a broadened and differentiated product line, Financing was likewise essential. Defining what was required in these Key Capabilities and then meeting those requirements provided the way for this company to undertake its major change in direction.

Not all organizations change their Driving Force. Many keep their current Driving Force but change its emphasis. Here again, the Driving Force shapes the supporting Key Capabilities. For example, one organization in both the downstream and upstream aspects of the petroleum business shifted from a petroleum-centered to an energy-centered NATURAL RESOURCES Driving Force. As a result, the organization needed significant growth in certain upstream activities. It also required the steady influx of substantial capital to support its new thrust and intensive research to develop new technology to exploit new forms of energy. Therefore, Production (refining) became less important and Financing and Technology became much more important than in the past.

Another organization was a regional producer of a popular soft drink. It had a PRODUCTS OFFERED Driving Force with a heavy emphasis on Production and Marketing capabilities. Top management met to consider future strategy. While this organization kept its PRODUCTS OFFERED Driving Force, it decided to duplicate its successful regional model on a national scale. This was to be done over a planned time frame, in a series of concentric circles that radiated from its regional base. Human Resources, both at general and functional management levels, Sales, and Distribution became Key Capabilities.

Size/Growth and Return/Profit Guidelines: Just about every organization uses financial and growth targets as a basis to plan and judge its results. However, such targets tend to be operational in nature. They presume a scope of products and a customer base. In addition, these targets are derived not from the possibilities and constraints implied by the organization's Driving Force, but rather are built up from a historical data base. They are then projected forward along with certain economic, technological and socio-political assumptions. These targets may result in giving current product and market "winners" the bulk of the organization's resources, whether or not that makes strategic sense. Or, it may mean that some of the "losers" are getting more of the corporate resources than they deserve, given the tendency for making overly optimistic projections. Conversely, newer or more experimental products or markets may get shortchanged in spite of their long-term strategic significance. In the absence of a clear strategic framework, such operational targets guide major decisions regardless of strategic considerations or consequences.

It is critical for an organization to have operational growth and return targets to guide day-by-day decision making. However, they in no way replace or can be equated with *strategic* Growth and Return Guidelines. Such Guidelines answer the questions: Given the future Driving Force, Product Scope, Market Scope and the Key Capabilities required, how much growth is suggested and is feasible over the next few years and what should its trend be? How much return is possible and what is its likely trend over the time frame of our future strategy? The answers to these questions yield not operational projections, but strategic guidelines or estimates within the framework of the organization's proposed strategy. If these growth and return estimates are grossly inadequate, then the entire strategy should be reevaluated. By "grossly inadequate" we mean that these growth and return estimates do not assure the organization's survival, do not provide a higher growth and return than that projected in current long-range plans, or do not offset the threat of likely competitive moves. No amount of long- and short-range operational planning or budget cutting can overcome a strategy that does not include sufficient growth and return estimates.

Strategically-set Size/Growth and Return/Profit Guidelines are statements about how quickly or slowly an organization should grow and about its return, given the intent of the Driving Force, Product and Market Scope, and Key Capabilities. For example, an organization that changes from a PRODUCTION CAPABILITY to a MARKET NEEDS Driving Force typically must make substantial resource commitments to its Marketing and Sales capabilities in the early stage of the implementation of its strategy. The intent of the strategy and these commitments is to produce a range of products that will better insure the organization's growth and survival as the strategy matures. This organization, therefore, must establish its strategic Size/Growth and Return/Profit Guidelines with this new emphasis and resource commitment in mind.

Business Unit Mission Statements to Guide Resource Allocation: The strategic allocation of resources is especially difficult when those resources must be apportioned among various product and market groups. We have found that in multi-product/market organizations, it is essential to include Mission Statements for business units in the organization's statement of corporate strategy. Otherwise, you risk having your strategy and your resources headed in different directions.

Mission Statements are bridges between the organization's corporate strategy and the strategies of business units and key staff departments. They are set by top management as part of the corporate statement of strategy, but they do not replace the need for these business units or staff groups to determine their own Driving Force and Strategic Framework. Rather, Mission Statements are the corporate guides to the strategies and plans which the units will be setting. They answer such questions as: Why is this business unit or staff group a part of this organization? What is its unique or major expected contribution to corporate strategy? And what, therefore, is its emphasis relative to other business units or staff groups?

The corporate Driving Force and the rest of the Strategic Framework are the basis for Mission Statements. Each unit's growth (or reduction), its unique contribution and the Key Capabilities it requires must be assessed in terms of the corporate Driving Force.

In the Mission Statement below, notice how the corporate strategy is used to guide the direction of a major business unit.

Mission Statement
SYNTHETIC MATERIALS BUSINESS
(Six-Year Time Frame)

Synthetic Materials çarries out the manufacturing and sales operations of all-synthetic materials, thereby supporting the increased emphasis on man-made materials mandated by the corporate PRODUCTS OFFERED Driving Force. It also develops the necessary technology for the creation of new synthetic products, consistent with the corporate Driving Force and Future Product Scope.

Synthetic's long-term growth rate and return to support corporate strategy should be:

	Growth Rate	Return
First and Second Year	_____%	_____%
Third and Fourth Year	_____%	_____%
Fifth and Sixth Year	_____%	_____%

Synthetic Materials is the source of cash flow to support the pay-your-own-way requirement of our corporate strategy. Therefore, Synthetics requires the cash flow generated from its operations. This includes the critical requirements for a well-trained staff of hourly, salaried and management personnel. Total staff level will grow from 1500 to 2500 over the next six years.

Just as Mission Statements are bridges between corporate strategy and the strategies of business units, they are also bridges to the strategies of staff groups. After all, staff groups have products or services to offer, markets or customers to serve, resources to allocate, and results to achieve. They too must come to terms with the Driving Force and Strategic Framework. In so doing, their efforts can best be guided by clearly formulated Mission Statements which relate the staff function to the corporate strategy.

One example of the relationship between a corporate strategy and the strategy of a staff group comes from a multi-national organization with a large Industrial Relations Department (IRD). This department had a substantial budget, a large number of skilled resources and a sense of mission that, in hindsight, often placed it at odds with the rest of the organization. The existing corporate strategy was simply too vague to provide the IRD with the needed guidance. "Our basic mission," read the IRD's charter, "is to provide the IRD's services to the management and employees of our organization to achieve optimum utilization of human resources."

This statement proved an illusive guide for the IRD. Without a clear sense of mission, it pursued what, in retrospect, can loosely be called a PRODUCTS OFFERED Driving Force. It spent considerable time developing an array of sophisticated, high-quality personnel policies, systems and programs which were marketed throughout the organization. There was only one difficulty: their efforts were put together without the benefit of a clear, explicit strategy. "There was a vacuum," explained the Director of IRD, "and we tried to fill it as best we could."

Once the corporation determined its Driving Force and defined the other dimensions of its Strategic Framework, the IRD's mission took on a much different meaning and a much sharper definition. Its reformulated Mission Statement began this way:

> This statement of mission defines corporate management as the user group. The IRD's primary focus is to find new and better ways to equip corporate and top functional management with the tools to manage and develop the organization's human resources. While IRD will continue to provide services to organizational units, these services will be derived from the major human resource development needs required by the corporate strategy.

The new Mission Statement represented a significant shift in focus for the IRD, one which would enable it to meet the strategy-oriented manpower needs of the organization. No longer would the IRD only develop and promote the myriad of day-to-day operational services which lacked cohesion and strategic focus. Rather, in line with the requirements of the corporate strategy, the IRD's mission became the transfer of defined skills to a specific user group which had a specific set of needs.

The Mission Statement then went on to identify corporate management's needs and to spell out the department's specific contribution to satisfying these needs. The IRD's level of growth over the time frame of the strategy, its major resource needs and key operational tactics to support the organization's Driving Force were planned in detail.

In addition, because the IRD's mission was clear and tied to the corporate Driving Force, it could then develop a strategy congruent with the corporate strategy.

This enabled the IRD to play a vital and exciting role in the organization. As the Director of the IRD put it, "before corporate management defined its strategy and our role, we were confused. We didn't have a clear understanding of our role. We didn't really know who our constituency was or what we really should be doing. So we did what we knew best how to do. Once we understood the organization's Driving Force and how we tied in, we could get a better handle on our primary user group, what had to be done to support it and how to go about getting the job done."

With a sharper statement of mission, the IRD was not only able to bridge into its own strategy, but it became a more effective unit and gained greater acceptance throughout the organization.

SOME COMMON MISCONCEPTIONS

Several misconceptions regularly surface when the concept of Driving Force is initially presented. Top managers often mistakenly make one of the following observations.

MISCONCEPTION: *"*RETURN/PROFIT *must be our Driving Force. That's why we're in business."*

Profit *is* essential. For most organizations, profit equates with survival. Profit is also a key indicator of success and an important yardstick by which organizations measure the effectiveness of their operations—and thus their strategy. But, as we have already seen, RETURN/PROFIT is a Driving Force only when it is the primary determinant of the scope of products and markets for that organization. In very few companies is this actually the case. In most companies, even though profit is critical as a measure for success and survival, the scope of products and markets is determined by one of the other Strategic Areas serving as a Driving Force. International Telephone and Telegraph is an example of a company whose actions strongly suggest a RETURN/PROFIT Driving Force. Its highly diversified products and markets are, for the most part, related only by the fact that they pass—or are expected to pass—minimum profitability or return requirements. Determining the Driving Force and the products and markets that it suggests is the best assurance that an organization will continue at rates of growth and profit that will enable it to survive in a rapidly changing and uncertain world.

MISCONCEPTION: *"Obviously,* RETURN/PROFIT *is our Driving Force. It's how we screen our prospective products and markets."*

Most organizations use a number of criteria to screen product and market choices. Return/profit is one such screen. Because return/profit considerations are used as a primary criterion to screen specific product and market choices does not necessarily mean that RETURN/PROFIT is the Driving Force. Consider a company that is contemplating an acquisition. This company should first ask, "Is the product line and customer base of this acquisition within our Driving Force and our Product and Market Scope?" If it is not, then the acquisition's profitability, excellence of management and the like, become interesting but irrelevant facts. The acquisition should not be considered further, *unless* it is of sufficient interest to suggest a change in Driving Force and, therefore, in corporate strategy. If the products and markets brought by the acquisition are within the intent of the Driving Force, Product Scope and Market Scope, then the company may well use profitability as the major criterion to determine whether it should proceed further or consider other alternatives. This organization should not deviate from its strategy even with an acquisition opportunity that shows a very favorable profit performance.

MISCONCEPTION: *"Once we set our Driving Force, we are stuck with it."*

The Driving Force is not permanently fixed. Changes in the environment, in the competitive picture, in internal capabilities or in the desires of top management can lead to a change in an organization's Driving Force. In fact, we have observed a number of companies changing their Driving Force. As you review our observations below think about the evolution of companies you know to see how they might have changed.

One such change is from a PRODUCTS OFFERED to a MARKET NEEDS Driving Force. For example, a company characterized by a PRODUCTS OFFERED Driving Force built a strong franchise with the customer group that bought its products. Over time, this company decided that it could fill other needs for the customer group it served. Eventually, it shifted to a MARKET NEEDS Driving Force.

Another type of change is from a MARKET NEEDS to a RETURN/ PROFIT Driving Force. A company developed the ability to do effective market research in a given market segment and to produce and sell a range of services accordingly. As it gained managerial expertise and control systems to handle this range of services, it sought to capitalize on those skills and penetrate new, unrelated markets. The company became RETURN/PROFIT-driven and over time, consciously diversified.

A third change we have observed is a shift from a PRODUCTS OFFERED Driving Force to a NATURAL RESOURCES Driving Force. For example, one company has a product line which uses a natural resource as a raw material. Over time, that resource became increasingly scarce. With its investment in the sources of that natural resource, the company began to look upon control of that natural resource as being more important than the particular product line which was made from it. The management of the company turned to NATURAL RESOURCES as a Driving Force. This Driving Force led to a wider range of products and markets that significantly utilized that natural resource as a raw material.

Finally, a fourth change is from PRODUCTION CAPABILITY to PRODUCTS OFFERED as a Driving Force. An organization with a commodity base built an extensive production capability. Product volumes were high, margins were often low. Over time, product sophistication was selectively improved. Through vertical integration, value-added increased by product. Growth, profitability and future promise for these products likewise increased. A market franchise was established. The organization shifted to a PRODUCTS OF-

FERED Driving Force and now molds its Production Capability accordingly.

While all the above examples show changes in Driving Force, for some organizations such changes are difficult and even painful to contemplate. Where a single product is unique, or capital intensity is high, or there is a concentration of a highly unique skill, changing Driving Force may be a long-term proposition. On the other hand, these barriers should not automatically obstruct top management consideration of alternative futures.

MISCONCEPTION: *"Even though our division's business is different, I guess it must have the same Driving Force as the Corporation."*

Not really. Take the International Telephone and Telegraph example mentioned earlier. While the company at the corporate level has a RETURN/PROFIT Driving Force, this is probably not true for any of its divisions. Having each division carefully determine its Driving Force from corporate Mission Statements is the best guarantee that the company's corporate return expectations will be met. Du Pont is another example. Corporately, it would appear to be TECHNOLOGY-driven. But, over the years its technology has produced numerous products which have then been developed into separate business units with different Driving Forces.

Many of today's organizations are engaged in a variety of businesses with highly divergent product and market activities. Provided that the Driving Forces of the business units complement each other and support the corporate Driving Force, it makes little sense to impose a uniform strategy on every aspect of the business. The corporate Driving Force serves both as a point of reference and a point of departure for business-unit strategies. Divisional or functional managers who recognize the corporate Driving Force and build their unit's strategy and operating plans accordingly know that all significant product, market and resource decisions across the company will be made first within that corporate framework. These managers have the freedom to concentrate on effectively implementing their divergent strategies within that corporate framework.

Diversity can be a source of strength when it is directed toward a common, corporate strategic goal.

MISCONCEPTION: *"The combination of two or more Strategic Areas is better for our organization than a single Driving Force."*

All of the nine Strategic Areas are vital to the survival of any organization. The Driving Force answers this question: Under the pressure of making product or market choices, which one of the Strategic Areas provides the final test for considering or not considering a potential product or market? That Area is the Driving Force and it is not negotiable. For example, there may be a fine line between PRODUCTION CAPABILITY and PRODUCTS OFFERED as the primary determinant of the scope of future products and markets. But ultimately, if you determine that PRODUCTS OFFERED is the final screen for product acceptance or rejection, then you are willing to modify your production capability to support that decision. If you determine that PRODUCTION CAPABILITY is the final screen for product acceptance or rejection, then that production capability determines your scope of products and their priority. If you combine Driving Forces, you have lost the concept.

MISCONCEPTION: *"The Driving Force is just another name for product emphasis, market emphasis, production emphasis and so on."*

Wrong. Just because an organization emphasizes certain skills or is known for a particular capability does not mean that those skills or that capability is the Driving Force. For years, Coca Cola was known for its worldwide marketing capability, yet it had a PRODUCTS OFFERED Driving Force. 3M has long been known for its excellence in management, but "management" is not its Driving Force. Pharmaceutical companies head the list of profit makers, yet RETURN/PROFIT is not their Driving Force. Xerox and Control Data Corporation have been characterized by rapid growth, but "growth" is not their Driving Force. Regardless of the "emphasis" or notoriety of a particular capability, that capability is the Driving Force only if it determines the scope of products and markets.

DRIVING FORCE: TRAJECTORY OF AN IDEA

The concept of Driving Force is fundamental to strategic thinking. It is the unifying concept for the Strategic Framework and it guides top management's deliberations in arriving at that Framework. Here is why:

- The essential nature of an organization is reflected in its products, the markets or customers it serves, its capabilities to support those products and markets, its growth and return, and its allocation of resources. The Driving Force gives definition to each of these areas of choice and integrates them into a coherent Strategic Framework.
- The concept of Driving Force provides the basic means for generating alternative futures and for assessing what each might mean in terms of products, markets, capabilities and return. It is common these days to talk of "future scenarios," "cross-impact analysis," "model building" and the like. These techniques to gain insight into the future may be useful but they are often needlessly complicated and are devoid of a link to strategy. The Driving Force provides a practical approach which top managers can "own" as they develop realistic alternative futures for their organization and discuss and evaluate their relative merits. In effect, this concept enables top managers to say, "If PRODUCTS OFFERED were our Driving Force, over time this is what we would look like." On the other hand, "If MARKET NEEDS were our Driving Force, this is what we would look like." The concept of Driving Force gives top managers a mechanism for developing, specifying and understanding the different futures which are possible for their organization. And, because the alternative futures that emerge are discrete, clear and vividly focused, they can be analyzed and tested against crucial aspects of that organization's internal and external environments to arrive at a future strategy.

- The Driving Force helps top management highlight and then resolve differences about the nature and direction of the organization. In looking at such variables as internal strengths and vulnerabilities, competition and external threats and opportunities, different managers can reasonably have different perspectives on what the organization's future Driving Force should be. Having to grapple with and ultimately determine the organization's Driving Force brings out these divergent opinions and helps management assess and deal with them to arrive at a clear, specific and useful statement of strategic direction.

- Without recognizing the Driving Force behind product and market decisions, it is difficult to consciously and systematically change the nature and direction of the organization. Ultimately, you must know *from what* you are changing. Unless the Driving Force is recognized and addressed, attempts to change an organization's direction will be very difficult or even futile.

- The concept of Driving Force is vital to the CEO who has a picture in mind of where the organization is headed, but cannot clearly articulate that picture so it can be shared with the top management team. The CEO's vision is imprinted in the decisions he makes, but *why* is not always apparent to others. One CEO gave this example:

> We had identified the need to break our business into segments. I was the one who initiated this approach. In the back of my mind I knew where I wanted the business to go: I could put the component parts together. I asked my subordinates to put together a plan. But when they presented the final plan to me, they complained, "We've done what you've asked us to do, but we don't know where we're going. How can we measure whether we're there or not? We need a handle that we haven't got right now on what the key objectives are for this business." The next time around, the concept of Driving Force provided that handle.

- Using the Driving Force to organize strategy sessions helps the CEO assess the thinking of key people on the most significant issues facing the organization. It also helps members of the top team to better understand the CEO and one another. Since the Driving Force penetrates to the essence of an organization, superficial and tangential discussion is controlled. The discussion is kept clear, specific and conclusive.

- The most skillfully formulated strategy will fail if that strategy cannot gain the understanding and commitment of key managers throughout the organization. The Driving Force keeps the statement of strategy simple, and gives it a unity and logical consistency that make its rationale easy to explain and its meaning easy to understand. Commitment comes when the strategy makes sense.

- The concept of Driving Force is also of great value in tracking competition. Since there is no way to know the actual strategy of your competitors, you can carefully observe their actions to gain insight into their Driving Force. The future product and market actions of a competitor will be easier to anticipate, once you make realistic assumptions regarding that competitor's Driving Force.

Stating the benefits of the Driving Force is one way to convey its usefulness. Another way is to take a random sampling of some tough situations top managers have faced and see how these situations were clarified and resolved by using the concept of Driving Force.

Situation: The No-Growth Future

The CEO of a single-product company became increasingly concerned about the near certainty that his organization faced a future of limited growth. Changes in consumer preferences diminished the likelihood that this organization would continue to grow in the near and long-term future. Senior management was equally concerned. Although the top managers all grew up in the business, they knew that changes had to be made. A task force was formed, headed by the CEO and advised by an outside consultant. The task force stalked the acquisition trail for over a year, searching for companies with new products. One year later searching, followed by intense discussion, continued but there was no firm action. "It's hard to act," said one task force member, "without guidance. The only thing we all agreed on was that our organization's current position was not adequate."

RESOLUTION

Centering their discussions around the concept of Driving Force helped to clarify the *real* strategic options available to this organization.

The CEO and his top managers developed a number of possible future Driving Forces. One possible Driving Force—the one, it turns out, they had been pursuing the past year—was RETURN/PROFIT. This Driving Force did not allow the organization any leverage with its real strengths and was quickly abandoned as unrealistic. Two other possible Driving Forces were assessed: PRODUCTION CAPABILITY and MARKET NEEDS. Each of these Driving Forces was carefully detailed and then analyzed.

As discussion continued, it became clear that the MARKET NEEDS Driving Force took greatest advantage of the organization's major unique strength: its image in its current market. The company sold its products through a number of outlets such as department stores and specialty shops. Although its high-quality image was related to a single product line, the top team felt confident it could parlay the organization's reputation into other products for the same market. A MARKET NEEDS Driving Force was the safest and soundest course for this organization.

Once the top team agreed that the future direction of the business was best served by a MARKET NEEDS Driving Force, they brought in a market research firm and an investment banker to help explore acquisition possibilities related to their existing market franchise and customer group.

With a clear sense of where they were going, these managers could better utilize the resources at their command. They could also bridge into the future realistically and confidently. They had come a long way from the previous year.

Situation: The House Divided

In a previous chapter, we discussed an organization that is an independent geographic distributor for a manufacturer of heavy construction equipment. The company was being pulled in a number of directions by key managers who tried to spin off a variety of new products and services, each of which presumed a different Driving Force and could become an independent business. Each key manager sought to define the future thrust of the organization in terms of his particular function. This organization realized it could no longer function as a house divided.

RESOLUTION

The concept of Driving Force enabled this organization to reaffirm its commitment to its current PRODUCTS OFFERED thrust. "We have agreed," stated the CEO, "that the Driving Force of our company has been and continues to be PRODUCTS OFFERED. This indicates that we are a company whose products are the prime consideration in determining our direction and the actions we take."

The top team clearly delineated the organization's Product Scope. "Our product characteristics clearly show that the equipment from our manufacturer is the primary product line." Products from other suppliers would be considered, provided they rounded out the line and "provided they could not be supplied by our manufacturer." In addition, only those services that "support the products we sell" would be pursued. Thus, the financial service, originally slated to become an independent business, was to remain an integral part of the current organization. Along with an expanded credit service, it would be supportive of the PRODUCTS OFFERED Driving Force. On the other hand, the decision to expand the product line to include competitors' vehicles was dropped. It threatened relationships with the primary manufacturer and was too great a risk to assume, given the Driving Force.

The Driving Force enabled this organization to get back to basics and to regain the commitment of top managers who had drifted into entrepreneurial opportunity seeking, independent of one another and of the larger organization.

Situation: Billion Dollar Diversions

A CEO described his situation this way: "Nobody at divisional level really had any idea or thoughts as to what the company's philosophy was toward what it wanted to be in the future. This was true because this philosophy had never been made clear at top levels of the company. I don't think those of us at the top ever got together and said what that philosophy was. At the divisional level, managers thought corporate policy might be to go out tomorrow to buy a widget factory. And sometimes we did. We bought a huge amount of raw material to make baseball bats, hardwood floors, etc. We got into the papermaking business for reasons that are still a mystery. The list of activities goes on and on. Such diversions cost us maybe a billion dollars." Without knowing it, this organization was pursuing a very expensive RETURN/PROFIT Driving Force.

RESOLUTION

The concept of Driving Force helped this organization to clarify what was behind past and present product and market decisions. This led to discussion of what should be driving the organization in the future. "We are not IT&T or GE," said the CEO, "and RETURN/PROFIT as a

Driving Force took us away from where we should be headed." And, where this company should be headed, these top managers concluded after examining a number of possible future Driving Forces, was "to stay within but significantly expand our primary business." For the future, it would pursue a PRODUCTS OFFERED Driving Force.

The Driving Force helped to set a tight boundary around what this organization should and should not be pursuing.

Situation: Groping At Growth

The division vice presidents of an organization involved in the exploration, refining and marketing of oil met with corporate officers to hammer out the organization's corporate strategy. Each division V.P. felt that the future of the organization rested squarely with the growth of his division. And each could persuasively argue for the lion's share of resources. How could these divergent opinions be reconciled? How should resources be allocated?

RESOLUTION

The word "growth" is susceptible to numerous interpretations. Casting the discussion in terms of the Driving Force helped each manager clearly express his understanding of how the organization should, in fact, "grow." Beyond clarity of expression, the concept of Driving Force became a tool by which diversity could be consolidated into a usable statement of strategy.

Thus, the Refining Department's concept of growth was reduced to the specifics of a PRODUCTION CAPABILITY Driving Force. It saw the organization's future tied to a substantially expanded and updated refining capability. The marketing department's desire to triple the number of service stations was given clearer definition when expressed as a PRODUCTS OFFERED Driving Force. The Exploration Department's desire to redirect its resources to support the search for new sources of supply, meant a NATURAL RESOURCE Driving Force should be adopted.

Each of these Driving Forces was carefully and comprehensively defined and then tested from a corporate viewpoint. In the process of examining each alternative, it became clear to everyone that without a steady and increased supply of crude oil, the rest of the organization would come to a grinding halt. A NATURAL RESOURCES Driving Force, with the emphasis on obtaining new sources of supply, was the key not only to the Exploration Department's survival but to corporate survival over the long term. Everyone agreed that funds had to be siphoned from the rest of the organization to support the efforts of the Exploration Department.

The Driving Force served as a mechanism for vividly portraying alternative future directions and for having divergent viewpoints converge into a pragmatic and workable corporate strategy.

These examples lead to one conclusion. Examining these situations in terms of the Driving Force kept the focus exactly where it belonged: on what should determine the organization's Product and Market Scope.

CONCLUSION

The Driving Force should not be confused with any number of ideas currently in circulation about an organization's strategy. When we talk about the Driving Force, we are not referring to such notions as: forward or backward integration, optimizing among current products, portfolio management, filling the gap, the need to diversify, an emphasis on marketing or on efficiency in production, and the like. In our judgment, all of these are alternatives or means which can be put at the service of a particular Driving Force. These approaches are not *strategic* in our sense of the term; they are operational mechanisms to help support the basic thrust—the Driving Force—of an organization.

The Driving Force and the Strategic Framework define what an organization wants to be. They also provide a basis for determining the strategy of business units, for long- and short-term planning efforts and for major operational decisions. But having a strategy is not a guarantee that it will be used. Even the clearest statement of strategy must be carefully integrated into an organization's operational activities. Chapter Five explores how to make strategy happen in your organization.

Making Strategy Happen

Strategic management is a continuing process. It begins with the formulation of strategy, continues on to implementation and then moves to a review and update of the strategy as conditions change both inside and outside the organization. Each aspect of strategic management is important, but nowhere is the perseverance of the top team tested more acutely than in the area of implementing strategy. Making strategy happen requires linking what the organization wants to become with how it should get there.

Determining an organization's Driving Force and then defining the Strategic Framework to support it is the toughest conceptual challenge facing top managers. Their responsibility for implementing that strategy is not so much a conceptual challenge as it is developing a discipline and methodology to put that strategy in place. While formulating strategy is the responsibility of top management alone, plans for implementing that strategy involve a coordinated effort between top management and a wide range of personnel throughout the organization. This chapter describes that discipline in some detail and suggests a supporting methodology.

A well-formulated strategy is the first step toward effective implementation. When a strategy statement is clear, simple and specific, it can be effectively communicated, remembered and used. Individual managers who can carry their organization's strategy in their heads are always "with it." Every plan that must be developed, every decision that must be made, can be tested against this mental picture. This is day-by-day implementation in its most basic and important sense.

Strategy must not only be clearly understood and applied by those who manage the business, it must also be built into the organization's structure. Mission Statements, as we have seen, build corporate strategy into the stated purpose of each business unit and staff department. Mission Statements and the strategies that evolve from them help create a strategic context for the organization and for those who manage it.

Yet, with all of this, there is a missing dynamic. We have found that making strategy happen requires the identification, management and resolution of what we call Critical Issues. This chapter will define and illustrate the Critical Issues approach to managing strategy. It will provide guidance on how this approach can be used in your organization.

THE CRITICAL ISSUES APPROACH TO MANAGING STRATEGY

A company we know started off years ago in a single-product natural resource business. The company was well managed, hired shrewd salesmen and marketers, and was strongly entrepreneurial in spirit. Business expanded and soon the organization was selling and delivering its raw material in markets all over the world. The company branched out, first increasing its processing capability and then, through its international subsidiaries, adding a wide array of products and services which included warehousing and shipbuilding, steel production and solid waste disposal, real estate management, and various financial services.

The organization's subsidiaries were relatively autonomous and, over time, each diversified and added to its own product line. For example, in one subsidiary, managers handling real estate became involved in the hotel business. In another, those handling transportation found themselves in truck rentals and leasing. These subsidiaries drifted far afield from the original basic business which remained this organization's single most important source of growth and profit.

Within the company, reporting relationships were characterized by an almost labyrinthine complexity. Some international subsidiaries reported to European headquarters while others, including a number of subsidiaries in Europe, reported to corporate headquarters in the U.S. Some product lines and plants within these subsidiaries reported to Europe and others, for no apparent reason, reported to the U.S.

The solid, sustained pattern of growth plus a bright profit picture bolstered the optimism of the top team, at least for the near-term future. Yet, when the top managers met and, for the first time, developed an explicit statement of strategy for the entire organization, a number of important and difficult questions arose. How do we make sure this strategy will guide our long-range reinvestment, acquisition and divestment efforts? What new policies and procedures do we need to keep management strategically focused? How can the complex network of reporting relationships be clarified so the organization's structure better supports the strategy? What will we do with the products and services that are outside the intent of our strategy?

The questions that this company raised are critically important to the success of the strategy. Without resolving these questions, the organization's operations could have continued to head in different directions, regardless of corporate desire.

These unresolved questions are typical of what we call Critical Issues. They relate to the linkages between strategy and operations. *Critical Issues are those major changes, modifications, additions to the organization's structure and systems, to its capabilities and resources, to its information needs and management that result from setting strategy.* And they must be resolved for strategy to succeed.

Some of these Issues may surface directly out of top management's deliberations on strategy formulation, for example, the need to monitor new competitors, the need for improved tracking of an environmental trend, the need to modify a basic belief of the organization. These might truly be called "Strategic Issues." Other Issues may surface more from the need to modify operations given a clear strategy. For example, the need to expand marketing of a current product, the need to further penetrate a particular market segment, the need to speed the implementation of a new information system. These might well be called "Operational Issues." Whether

Issues are "Strategic" or "Operational" in theory, if they are critical to the success of the strategy, then in practice they must be resolved. They are important action items on the agenda of strategy implementation.

THE SOURCES AND RANGE OF CRITICAL ISSUES

Where you look for Critical Issues and the number you find are a function of two main factors:

1. The extent to which the future Driving Force is different from the current Driving Force. For example, an organization going from a METHOD OF DISTRIBUTION to a MARKET NEEDS Driving Force can expect Critical Issues in all the key Strategic Areas and Capabilities, to say nothing of organization structure, the external environment and competition.
2. The overall health and strength of the organization. For example, an organization with very few unique strengths, with shortages of capable management or with a weak franchise in its markets may find itself faced with significant Critical Issues, regardless of a change in Driving Force. Here, the very act of setting strategy brings Critical Issues to the surface.

Within each of these main sources, additional Critical Issues may emerge. Some Issues surface because a strategy may be confronted by an external threat. For example, pending government regulations or restrictions, demands by various interest groups, or a potential breakthrough by a competitor may pose hazards to the health of the strategy. While the seriousness of such threats may not be sufficient to cause a change in strategy, their potential impact must be managed as Critical Issues.

Sometimes, Critical Issues emerge when a division or a business unit considers its strategy in relationship to the overall corporate philosophy. In one subsidiary, for example, perhaps the most pressing Critical Issue centered around the fact that its strategy ran counter to a basic belief of the parent organization's. The corporate board of directors viewed the subsidiary as a "cash cow" whose major function was the cost-effective conversion of raw materials to finished products for sale to the U.S. market, thereby generating cash to support other corporate ventures. When the subsidiary developed a PRODUCTS OFFERED Driving Force with parallel needs for heavy front-end investment in product development and marketing, a pressing Critical Issue became: How do we convince the board to modify its perspective, given where we want to be five years out?

Some Critical Issues may emerge because a new Driving Force has an impact on a unique strength of an organization. A PRODUCTS OFFERED-driven company with a very specialized product line reviewed its strategy and with its strong market franchise decided to shift to a MARKET NEEDS Driving Force. One of this company's unique strengths had been its highly specialized and experienced sales organization and staff. The size, competency and specialized skill of this sales force made it a unique strength for the organization. The shift to MARKET NEEDS raised several Critical Issues regarding this unique strength. For example, What are we going to do with "good ol' Clyde"? How much of the sales force can be retrained to handle the broader range of products? How do we accomplish that training? What can we do to prevent an exodus of our "stars" to the competition?

Critical Issues have a pervasive presence. They can emerge at almost any juncture within the strategy setting process. For example, prior to setting its future strategy, the top team of a regional bank with international interests had to first determine its current strategy. When discussion centered on defining the current Market Scope, the CEO raised a question about risk. "How do we currently determine whether or not a potential new market outside the U.S. has a favorable risk/return ratio? What are our criteria?" Intensive discussion followed but not agreement. It was clear this was an Issue requiring attention, especially if the future strategy included international expansion.

Not all organizations change their Driving Force. In one company, for example, no bright and shiny new Driving Force emerged from the top team's efforts to set strategy. Nor did this company discover that its overall health and strength needed treatment. Its strategy-setting experience reinforced the soundness of its current PRODUCTS OFFERED Driving Force as the best course for the future.

The CEO of this company initially felt let down because no exciting new Driving Force or Critical Issues were identified. But that was just his initial reaction. Keeping the same basic product mix and relatively narrow focus led this CEO and his top managers to search within their structure for those sub-set Issues which would keep their organization's products and capabilities on the leading edge. Should we extend our product mix? Where should we position our products in the market? What levels of quality should we offer? Is our current marketing and sales approach through distributors best for the future?

This CEO found that even when his organization's look at strategy served to reinforce the soundness of what it was currently doing, the focus of the Driving Force still brought Issues to the surface which, while not "aha!"'s, required thoughtful study and resolution.

The range of Critical Issues that emerges from setting strategy may vary considerably from one organization to another. However, Critical Issues tend to cluster around several common areas. Let us examine some of these in detail.

The Alignment of Business Units: Once corporate strategy is set, business units or product/market groups within the organization may have to be emphasized or deemphasized, reorganized or regrouped. To illustrate, let us assume that a company had been operating without a clear strategy. It explicitly determined its future strategy only to discover that it has acquired certain companies or products or markets that do not fit within the intent of its strategy. This leads to Critical Issues centering on how to adapt or disengage. For example, given its Driving Force, one organization defined its future Product Scope as centering on a range of products providing for the transmission, distribution and conversion of electrical energy. This put the retail chain the organization had previously acquired—under a presumed "growth" strategy—outside the framework of the strategy it set. Consequently, one Issue the organization had to tackle was: What do we do with a potentially profitable, but strategically irrelevant, dollar- and time-consuming business unit?

Or, a company may find that it must significantly change the emphasis on certain products or markets, given a clear, focused strategy. How to accomplish this becomes a Critical Issue. Thus, one company was organized along geographic lines. Regional units served customer needs associated with complete ranges of products and services. The Driving Force and strategy, however, required the formation of company-wide product line groups. A number of Critical Issues emerged about how to reorganize and reposition the product and market groups to best support the new strategy. In other cases, the reverse is true. A product line structure is in place, but the strategy demands an organization focused more on serving markets, either on a geographic or industry basis. Again, Critical Issues emerge about how reorganization should proceed.

Communications: Communicating strategy involves much more than talk. There are numerous pitfalls or Issues which must be resolved for the strategy to be effectively communicated. For example, in some instances executives argue with good reason that to fully communicate the organization's strategy is to court disaster. Thus, one CEO has a five-year strategy which, when it is fully implemented, will mean severe disruption to a major subsidiary. He does not want to rock the boat prematurely. An energy company thought it wiser not to publicize its strategy because it would become a sitting duck for regulatory agencies.

Such reservations have merit. Discretion may indeed be the better part of valor. Fully communicating strategy may not always be in the best interest of the organization, especially where that strategy is sensitive. Each situation has its own constraints. There is no one formula guiding how much strategy to communicate. However, where limitations are put on communications, those limitations must be carefully considered. They may not only handicap a manager's ability to keep decisions consistent with the overall strategy, but they may erode commitment to the organization.

In other instances the Critical Issues flow more from how to get the strategy fully communicated, understood and applied across the organization. Failure to resolve these Issues may lead to misunderstanding and even resentment. In one company, for example, a division vice president had succeeded in welding a group of marginal companies into a profitable entity, fully realizing that he would need extensive capital outlays sometime in the near future to complete his efforts. Once the first phase was accomplished, the executive then turned in a plan and a capital-intensive budget for moving his organization toward further growth. When the president pointed out that the capital-intensive policy was counter to corporate strategy the subordinate felt betrayed by his own success. "If we had clearly communicated our strategy," the president observed, "we would not have run into this situation. Had the vice president known this aspect of our strategy, he would have devoted his energies to more productive long-term activities."

Regardless of where you are on the strategy-communication continuum, from significant discretion to full disclosure, Critical Issues about communication must be allowed to surface and be resolved. What should be communicated about the strategy and where and when should it be said? How much should be said and to whom? Stockholders? Middle Managers? Supervisors? Employees? Union leaders? Customers? Government? What forms should the communications take? Who should do the communicating?

These questions seem relatively straightforward, but recall the situation mentioned earlier in which a corporate strategy meant severe disruption to a major subsidiary. The communications Critical Issue was a dominant concern for this organization's top team. And, for the subsidiary that had to convince its board that it could no longer be viewed as a "cash cow," the very existence of its strategy hinged on effectively communicating it.

In one sense, behavior is the most important form of communication. The organization's "body language" can be a visible indicator of the level of commitment to its strategy. With a clear statement of strategy, a critical eye develops toward such questions as: Why was this major market decision made on the basis of comparing available alternatives, with no mention of the strategic implications? As presented, why is this division's plan apparently counter to the strategy we set? Why is there no apparent discussion of strategy in our product planning meetings? The lack of strategic emphasis in important discussions and decisions can itself become a Critical Issue.

When you have clearly formulated strategy with your top team, shared that strategy with those who need to know, tested their understanding, and made sure that strategy is the basis for what happens in the organization—when strategy becomes part of the operation's working dialogue, particularly audible whenever plans are formulated or key decisions are being made—you are success-fully managing the communications Critical Issue.

Resource Capabilities: Few would argue with the proposition that of all the assets a company commands, none is more important than the strengths and the capabilities of its human resources. Given the right people, you can do almost anything.

Because human resources are so vital to the success of strategy, it is not surprising that a number of Critical Issues are generated in areas such as staffing, manpower planning and reward. Once strat-egy is formulated the question emerges: To what extent must each of these areas be redirected as a result of the strategy?

Critical Issues frequently surface because of the relationship be-tween the Driving Force and the adequacy of human resources within an organization. Existing resources may be insufficient or inadequate to support the Driving Force that has been set. Or, a new Driving Force may make particular resource capabilities that have been of critical importance in the past less important in the future.

A department store had all but decided to purchase a chain of unisex clothing boutiques in support of its newly determined MAR-KET NEEDS Driving Force. As the impending decision came under review, again and again the top team returned to the nagging Issue of human resources. With a paper-thin management layer in the basic business, how would the new venture be managed? Siphoning off resources from their department-store business would be akin to robbing Peter to manage Paul. The potential to the department store for severe dislocation was high. Given the organization's human resource limitations, the top team began to question the wisdom of its new Driving Force. Some managers suggested that a return to the PRODUCTS OFFERED Driving Force was more realistic, at least for the next several years. Ultimately, the MARKET NEEDS focus held fast, even though a number of Critical Issues now had to be faced: How do we upgrade the management that comes with the boutique acquisition? What is our plan for shifting key managers from the department store to the boutique business? How do we build the kind of management depth that will allow us to continue to exploit this MARKET NEEDS Driving Force?

"We've always stressed manufacturing excellence, volume and

meeting delivery deadlines,'' said the CEO of an organization in the specialty chemical business. ''No one here ever heard much about marketing excellence; it's been, 'Pound the devil out of those plants and get the product out at lowest cost.' '' When the top corporate managers met to set strategy, they concluded that a more rifleshot approach to the market was needed, one which identified major current brand-name products with high potential. Going from a PRODUCTION CAPABILITY to a PRODUCTS OFFERED Driving Force meant, among other things, redirecting the organization's manpower. How do we build a first-rate sales and marketing team? What new capabilities in product development and market research do we require to support this Driving Force? What changes are needed in our management capabilities?

Of all the Critical Issues to surface in the human resources area, one of the toughest involves handling the situation in which a member of the top team, for whatever reason, finds it difficult to commit himself to the strategy that has been set. For example, the chairman and the president of one company could not agree on a future Driving Force. The president temporarily suspended his point of view and a strategy was tentatively formulated. But the cleavage between the two persisted. In such a situation, agreement must eventually be reached, even at the price of one side capitulating. Otherwise, there can be no commitment to a common sense of direction. More typically, a key manager may find that his unit has been deemphasized as a result of the strategy or that he is ''without portfolio,'' given the strategic need to combine his unit with others. It is at this juncture that a Critical Issue emerges, one that pits the need to retain the talents of a high-level contributor against the requirement to maintain commitment to the strategic direction. This is a very personal Critical Issue for the top man.

The External Environment: No man—and no organization—is an island. Or, to update the metaphor, we live in what one economist has called the ''spaceship earth.'' Our planet has become a closed system, in which an action—even one as apparently insignificant as misreading the gauges at Three Mile Island—can reverberate throughout the extremities of that system. Top management must take over the responsibility for environmental scanning so that the end result of such effort is useful information for strategy formulation.

Knowledge of what is taking place beyond an organization's boundaries is essential for survival. Some organizations, however, behave as though they exist in a vacuum. A chain of retail shoe stores located in the downtown areas of several cities in the northeastern United States continued to sell its high-priced shoes, oblivious to the social and economic changes that had taken place in its markets. Volume declined regardless of price cuts and profit margins shrank to a dangerous level. The top team did not fully appreciate the strategic dimensions of the downward spiral, until they tested the current Product Scope and Market Scope against the backdrop of the changing urban environment.

With a clear understanding of its Driving Force the top team becomes more sensitive to the impact of the external environment. An oil company set its corporate strategy and knew it also had to resolve a Critical Issue: "How can we gain a better understanding of our socio-political environment?" "How can the tracking of potential government activities that could affect us be improved?" The top team's interest in the subject represented more than a rekindling of enthusiasm for high school civics. By keeping its NATURAL RESOURCES Driving Force, this company would be increasingly subject to government pressures.

When an organization changes its Driving Force, new environmental Issues surface. What economic, technological and socio-political trends and changes should we monitor? What information is required? What are the relevant information sources—inside and outside the organization? How should that information be collected and interpreted? How should top management be involved in and direct this process?

This last question brings to mind a story told to us by a senior administrator/planner at a major U.S. automobile firm. His primary function was to gather data about the environment for planning purposes. Consequently, he attended all major futurist seminars, read all the appropriate literature and talked with opinion leaders in the field. He had accumulated file drawers of information on numerous environmental trends covering the next twenty years and beyond. "How," we asked, "was all this information used?" "In two ways," came the response. The planning staff, we were told, used the information to test the validity of long-range planning assumptions. Second, the information was used by several staff groups including research and development, finance and government relations. But the information was never provided to top management for strategic purposes. This administrator neither had access to top management, nor was there a mechanism in place to bring strategically relevant information to the attention of the top team.

That auto company is not alone. Several years ago, a colleague of ours talked with a number of futurist organizations to determine how well the information they painstakingly gathered influenced the direction of their client organizations. A chief concern of these futurists was what can be termed "information indifference." That is, a sizable number of organizations did not appear to take advantage of the information that they were receiving.

Futurists aside, there is more information about the external environment available *within* organizations than they use. From the board of directors to the planning staff to the sales force, organizations are literally storehouses of useful information about the external world. Yet, just about every top management team we have met has felt the need to improve its understanding of the external environment. Information that does exist is simply too fragmented, not sufficiently separated from strategic versus operational considerations, and difficult to retrieve when needed.

Top management must get involved in these Critical Issues: It must determine what specific and selective environmental information is required for formulating strategy. It must also set up a mechanism to see that this information is collected, analyzed and presented so that the top team can easily and effectively use it for determining a future Driving Force.

When an organization sets its strategy, it puts into motion a series of actions that, inevitably, will have impact beyond the organization's borders. Somewhere along the path of implementing strategy, organizations will have to face environmentalists, consumer advocates, equal opportunity demands, health and job safety requirements, and the like. Even the most skillfully devised strategy cannot keep a safe enough distance from all threats, or take advantage of all of the opportunities available in the external environment. Consequently, where the organization's strategy and the external environment interact is a fertile ground for Critical Issues.

Critical Issues related to the external environment can become real tests of the soundness of an organization's strategy. A plastics company with a limited product line and a PRODUCTS OFFERED

Driving Force faced a bleak future. The escalating costs of its oil-based raw materials put this organization in a long-term cost/price squeeze that eventually would have been intolerable. In addition, many of the key managers felt that government policy on the allocation of oil reserves would work against plastics, especially where less oil-dependent alternatives were available. The last straw came when customers balked at the latest price rise, one described by the CEO as "a modest proposal, considering the skyrocketing cost of raw materials." The CEO called in his top managers. "Okay," he said, "we can't convince our customers on our price change. We know our product line is becoming increasingly more vulnerable. Right now, we have a good business with a respectable growth rate. We need to address some tough questions. What can we do with our price-cost-profit relationship? Can we make it with this strategy? What's happening to this industry? What's happening to technology?" As it turned out, a study of these Critical Issues centering on the external environment forced a wholesale review of the strategic direction of the business.

The external environment is vast and nebulous and impossible to scan without coordinates. Tracking everything from acts of God to the actions of government entities, pressure groups and the competition, not to mention iron laws of economics and of nature, can be expensive. A bank with significant international interests viewed "environmental forces" as its most important Critical Issue. The bank's strategy could be significantly affected by the "fragility of the international finance system," as well as all those forces associated with being in a sluggish Federal Reserve District. Where should the bank's scanning efforts be concentrated?

The Driving Force provided the bank with the focus it needed. The bank knew that its principal scanning activities should center on identifying and tracking those international business trends likely to affect customers with substantial business interests abroad. It would also consider selected slices of national and international political reality to determine how those realities might influence both the bank's customers and the bank's willingness to make loans for foreign business ventures. The Driving Force provided direction for the resolution of Critical Issues in environmental scanning.

PROBING FOR CRITICAL ISSUES

The sources for Critical Issues arise from a broad spectrum. Identifying Issues for any particular strategy requires a way to "dig in." These questions have proven useful:

- What changes in the organization's structure are suggested?
- What changes are needed in the organization's long- and short-term planning process and plans?
- What is the significance of the future strategy to current management skills?
- What new capabilities and resources will be required?
- How should strategy be communicated?
- What current strengths, capabilities, products and markets will require a change in priority or emphasis?
- What are the implications for current beliefs, policies, procedures and systems?
- What are the consequences of under-utilizing current strengths not required by the future strategy?
- What is the impact of the future strategy on competition?
- What would be the consequences of any external threats or internal vulnerabilities that are not addressed by the future strategy?
- How can we more effectively track the external environment?

MANAGING CRITICAL ISSUES

Systematically identifying Critical Issues is the first step in implementing strategy. A second step is to put these Issues in priority so top management can concentrate its efforts where it really counts. Next, each Critical Issue must be carefully detailed. This means clarifying an Issue so that it cannot be misunderstood, then assigning responsibility so that it cannot be ignored and, finally, giving it a time frame so that it cannot be put off indefinitely. We have used the following questions to clarify Critical Issues:

- What, specifically, is the Critical Issue? How will you know it has been resolved?
- Who has primary accountability for resolving and recommending action on this Issue? Who else should be involved? Who will approve the recommended action?
- What are the *major* steps to resolution?
- When should progress be reviewed?
- When should the Issue be resolved?

Once Critical Issues have been detailed, an organizational mechanism must be developed to pull those Critical Issues together so they can be managed. However, the last thing most organizations need is another committee. Every organization already has a forum for top management discussion and review. We have found that the best way to handle Critical Issues is to build them directly into this established top management forum.

Finally, a method by which top management can systematically review Critical Issues is needed. The Critical Issues Agenda is one alternative that works. It is a list of high-priority Issues, the personnel accountable for those Issues, a plan for their resolution and suggested time frames.

One CEO had this to say in explaining the Critical Issues Agenda:

> During our strategy session, we identified and detailed no fewer than twenty-five Critical Issues. After the session, we kept those Issues— and the ones that developed subsequently—in front of our top managers by circulating the Critical Issues Agenda and making it a basis for our executive committee meetings.
>
> Keeping these Issues in circulation creates pressure to get them resolved. Some of the Issues are mine to handle and when I don't deliver, I get questioned just like anyone else. There's nowhere to hide.
>
> The Critical Issues Agenda serves as a channel along which information about an Issue flows. Those besides top management who receive a copy of the Agenda are free to comment on an Issue.
>
> Everyone contributes, once you give them a means to do so. This not only improves the quality of the resolution of Issues, but it also insures key management commitment to the strategy.

The following is a sample Critical Issues Agenda. The Issues shown are taken from a number of such Agendas.

CRITICAL ISSUES AGENDA
EXECUTIVE COMMITTEE (EC)
1 January 19——

Issue	Responsibility
1. Develop and implement a program to insure that our long-range planning process is conducted within the context of the corporate strategy.	Task Force: *Executive V.P.* V.P. Finance Dir. Administration Dir. Planning
2. Develop and implement a plan to phase out —— product which falls outside our strategy.	*V.P. Finance* Sales Manager Production Manager Personnel Manager
3. Develop a long-range manpower plan to provide sufficient, competent, general management to support the direction and growth of our strategy.	*V.P. IR* Dir. Planning Personnel Manager Div. Personnel Mgrs.
4. Develop an environmental scanning approach for tracking federal legislation.	*Dir. Corporate Affairs* Dir. Public Relations Legal Counsel Dir. Planning

Steps	Time Frame
1. Develop and implement a program to insure that corporate strategy is understood by those involved in long-range planning.	January–February
2. Develop a mechanism enabling line managers to integrate strategy with long-range planning.	March
3. Brief EC prior to long-range planning cycle.	15 April Meeting
4. Develop a set of questions and a methodology by which top management can assess the strategic implications of long-range plans.	May
5. Implement Step 4 during plan approval, EC	June
6. Assess plan progress, EC	Quarterly
1. Develop action plan for two year phase-out with contingencies to protect customer credibility and human resources.	January–May
2. Review/approval, EC	15 May Meeting
3. Begin implementation	June
4. Progress review, EC	15 July Meeting 15 October Meeting 15 January Meeting
1. Take stock of current quantity and quality of general management.	January
2. Project requirements for general management over future strategic time frame.	February
3. Formulate a long-range plan to acquire and develop needed general management.	March
4. Approval, EC	15 April Meeting
5. Build long-range and first year program into corporate and divisional planning process.	By 1 July
6. Provide biannual progress reviews, EC	15 October Meeting 15 May Meeting
1. Assess current tracking system, information and deficiencies.	January
2. Develop action plan including: what should be tracked, sources, collection and interpretation and format for presentation.	February–March
3. Review/approval, EC	15 April Meeting
4. Implement plan.	May–October
5. Present information to EC in preparation for strategy update.	20 November

In this sample Critical Issues Agenda, we have obviously "planted" four Issues which frequently surface when strategy is being implemented. Because these Issues are so pervasive, an additional comment on each would be helpful.

We included the first Issue on planning because of our strong belief that long-range planning must be separated from strategy formulation. At this Critical Issue phase, both must be brought together and related. Planning provides the bridge between strategy and day-to-day operational decision-making. Given this, it is top management's responsibility to see that:

1. The corporate strategy and the mission statements for each function are understood by all managers with a responsibility for planning.
2. Plans are developed and approved by careful testing against the strategy.
3. Major operational decisions first satisfy the requirements of the strategy and then meet relevant operational criteria.

Once the Issue on planning is resolved, it can be deleted from the Critical Issues Agenda. The bridge between strategy and operational planning has been built.

Critical Issue number two—discontinuing products (or markets) that fall outside the strategy—is tough and knotty. Almost as difficult is handling those products or markets that are to be deemphasized. The Driving Force, as we have seen, determines an organization's Product and Market Scope. Organizationally, this means that certain business units or product and market groups will receive less emphasis than others. Few managers welcome the eclipse of their area. Sensitivity in managing this Issue is, therefore, crucial. The "phase out" or deemphasis Issue is the kind that might be on the Critical Issues Agenda for a long period of time.

The third Critical Issue deals with human resource planning on a long-term basis. Given the press of daily operational activity, this Issue is often shunted aside until a crisis brings it forward. Then it may be too late to take effective action. Human resource Critical Issues are not readily susceptible to eleventh-hour fire fighting. Top management has the unique responsibility to make sure that, over the long term, human resources are being developed to meet the needs of the organization's strategy. This Critical Issue requires thoughtful and periodic monitoring by top management.

Critical Issue number four—improving environmental scanning —is one that even the most sophisticated organizations have not fully resolved. The Issue in our example focuses on the need to improve the quality and flow of information about pending legislation. Other organizations have expressed a need to develop better information channels to track competition, technological developments, changes in economic and social conditions, shifts in natural-resource availability, and the like. While environmental scanning is of growing significance, top managers have tended to shy away from it. Typically, responsibility for tracking environmental information is farmed out to a number of departments. Corporate or public affairs tracks government; research and development monitors technology; sales and marketing focus on competition; finance and the economists study and predict economic developments. All of this information is brought together in the planning function. Often, this results in a system which is operationally focused and, therefore, of marginal utility to top managers who must review and update the strategy. Top management must take the responsibility for a strategically relevant environmental scanning system.

KEEPING TRACK

The Issues that are candidates for the Critical Issues Agenda are those that bear directly on the implementation of strategy. Without their resolution, it is unlikely the strategy will be successfully implemented and maintained. Contrast these Issues to the myriad of operational problems and decisions that face managers daily, for example, determining a "promote from within" policy; replacing depreciated equipment; coping with ERISA-type requirements; considering alternative compensation and incentive plans; improving operating efficiencies. All these may be important, but they typically do not relate to managing and implementing strategy.

The Critical Issues Agenda is dynamic. As long as the strategy is in place, Critical Issues surface and are resolved, only to be replaced by new Issues, which again demand analysis and resolution. This is the typical pattern. But not all Issues can, in fact, be permanently resolved. One organization, for example, is particularly vulnerable to patent infringements. As the CEO explained, "the infringement Issue is one which we're never going to really resolve. It's ongoing. I don't think we'll ever take it off the Agenda." Such an Issue must be monitored and reviewed on a continuing basis.

The Agenda is dynamic in another sense. As Issues are reviewed by top management, part of that review involves assessing whether any of those Issues suggest an extension, modification or change in strategy. Some Issues may have that level of impact: a major unexpected environmental threat, a radically new technology, a significant expansion by a competitor, highly restrictive government legislation, sudden loss of the company president, failure of a major new product thrust. Can these Issues be effectively resolved within the current strategic framework? Such Issues test the validity of the organization's strategy and serve to remind managers that strategy is not immutable. The tension set up, on the one hand, by the strategy and, on the other, by an Issue which may require a strategic adjustment, indicates that the organization's strategy is at the vital center of the top team's deliberations.

CONCLUSION

At the beginning of this chapter we said that strategic management is a continuing process. Strategy is formulated, it is implemented and then it is updated and, perhaps, reformulated. Strategy, in other words, must be carefully integrated into the thinking of managers, into the organization's structure and processes and into the way key issues are resolved. Otherwise, strategy will simply not "happen."

Beyond this, the successful implementation of strategy requires the top team to look deeply at itself, at the basic premises which govern its actions and which underlie the key management functions of the organization. This act of critical introspection poses a number of challenges for strategic managers. These challenges will be discussed in our sixth and final chapter.

CHAPTER SIX

The Challenges of Strategic Management

Strategic thinking has consequences. Strategy, as we have defined it, is a framework which guides those choices which determine the nature and direction of an organization. Once that framework is clearly set, an organization can lay plans, marshal its resources and make its day-to-day decisions in light of what it wants to be. An organization can command its future.

Strategy, however, is not a panacea. It cannot guarantee success, nor can it promise deliverance from all the risks inherent in managing a business in an age of uncertainty. In fact, having set strategy, an organization is confronted with a number of important and unresolved challenges which must be addressed.

These are not Critical Issues to be placed on a Critical Issues Agenda. Rather, they are broad challenges which require considerable experimentation and hard thinking by top management. While much has been written and professed about these challenges, in our experience and judgment they basically remain unresolved and will continue to be until top management takes them personally and firmly in hand. For this reason, they are part of this book.

These challenges raise a number of questions which cut across every facet of the organization for which top management has strategic responsibility: the board of directors, the system for developing and rewarding key contributors, the planning function, the environment, the international organization, business units, the organization's "sacred cows" or implicitly held beliefs, longer-range "strategy beyond strategy," and the organization as a strategic "whole."

By identifying and defining the key challenges that continue to confront strategic managers in each of the above areas, we hope to pinpoint certain aspects of the practical application of strategy that need further thought and research.

CHALLENGE: DEFINING THE ROLE OF THE BOARD OF DIRECTORS IN THE STRATEGIC PROCESS

If strategy is to guide the organization, then it certainly must guide what by law, if not actual fact, is the organization's key governing body, the board of directors. There are two key questions that demand attention about the strategy-board relationship. First: To what extent should the board participate in setting strategy? Second: How can board discussion, review and decision making be kept strategically focused?

In terms of the first question, there are several roles a board can play. The board can be the co-partner of the top management team and participate in the formulation of strategy. If the board is drawn predominantly from the "inside," this is the role it would most likely play. Or, the board can act as an information source and a critical sounding board for the top management team during the strategy-setting process. This is typically the role given a predominantly "outside" board. Outside board members serve as the organization's window to the world. These board members, often drawn from a variety of fields, can be called upon to assist in strategy setting by providing the top team with valuable inputs and critiques.

It is difficult, perhaps impossible, to define the one best strategic role for the board to play, at least in the abstract. There is simply too much variety in the functioning and makeup of boards. Consequently, each role has its own advantages and drawbacks, depending on how the board is constituted and the relationship between the board and the top management team. Where boards are drawn primarily from outside the organization, it probably makes little sense to have the board serve as a co-partner in setting strategy. But the varied backgrounds of board members can be used to gain insights into the external environment; their unique perspectives can be used to assess the viability of alternative strategies; their critical abilities can be used as a final test of the soundness of the strategy set by the organization's top managers. Finally, as the watchdog of the organization, the board can be used to measure the performance of the top team against the strategy it has set.

Whether a board is drawn primarily from inside or outside the organization, it can and should contribute to the organization's strategy. This requires carefully thinking through the kind of contribution the board can realistically make and then structuring the board's efforts accordingly.

In terms of the second question we raised, top management must keep the board strategically focused. Many boards become steeped in operational discussions. This may be the result of a lack of strategic awareness on the board's part. Often it is a result of the board's trying to be helpful to management, or its understanding of how best to meet its obligation to stockholders. Just as often, top management draws the board into operational discussions. A division may be in trouble operationally. Management becomes preoccupied with fire fighting and looks to the board for guidance, or for support as an ally, or to keep it informed rather than risk springing an important operational problem on it as a complete surprise. In so doing, the top team may reason: What better way to utilize the board is there than to keep it informed and seek its counsel?

Answering the above question is not a matter of deciding whether or not the board should engage in operational discussions. Boards must review major operational problems, plans and recommendations. Our only concern is that the board's discussion of such operational issues proceed from the vantage of the organization's strategy.

Keeping board discussion and decision making strategically focused is becoming progressively more difficult to accomplish, given the independence of some boards, the lack of standard management controls over boards, and the growing practice of having spokesmen from various interest groups participate on boards. Added to this, multinational organizations are moving toward having broader cultural and geographical representation on their boards, based on the locations where revenues and profits are generated.

Understandably, these difficulties are especially acute in organizations that draw heavily upon "outsiders" for board membership.

In such organizations, it is the responsibility of the CEO himself to bridge the gap between the strategy that top management has set and the use of that strategy as a basis for board deliberations.

Keeping the board strategically focused is a real challenge, but there are ways to approach it. For example, in a number of organizations with predominantly outside board membership, we have seen CEOs carefully lay plans to heighten the awareness of strategic thinking among board members. These CEOs have made an effort to alert the board to the separation between strategy and long-range planning, and to enhance board understanding of strategy by taking the board through the logic of the Driving Force. This has made the board's critique of the strategy more incisive and the board's acceptance of that strategy more than *pro forma* approval. These CEOs have also encouraged board members to raise questions about the organization's strategy as an integral part of the board's conduct of its business.

At a somewhat different level, some CEOs circulate the Critical Issues Agenda to board members to remind them of top management's continuing commitment to review major concerns within the Strategic Framework. In one company, a CEO examined a number of board activities, trying to tie these closer to the organization's strategy. Thus, he took the lead in developing strategic performance criteria for the board to use in succession planning. This enabled the board to assess candidates for top positions not only against operational considerations but also against the strategic results the organization wanted to achieve.

All of this means that keeping the board strategically focused requires real effort, especially on the part of the CEO.

CHALLENGE: DEVELOPING AND REWARDING STRATEGIC THINKING AND ACCOMPLISHMENT

"By their fruits ye shall know them." For most organizations, the "fruits" by which managers are known and rewarded are primarily in the realm of operations. For them, the biblical injunction might better be restated, "By your operational accomplishments shall ye managers be rewarded."

Most managers advance in the organization because they have been successful operationally. This is no surprise. Financial incentives and career paths reflect the fact that the bulk of a manager's time and effort is spent in the day-to-day operations of the business. Equally no surprise.

Just as predictable is the fact that once managers reach the top positions in their organization, they continue to be operationally focused. After all, their careers have been made on the strength of operational achievement. So why switch now? Many managers, therefore, unknowingly face a disturbing dilemma. Their new responsibilities require an understanding of what strategy is, how it can be set and managed. Yet their frame of reference continues to be operational.

All of the above suggests that the experiences provided to upwardly mobile managers require re-evaluation. As managers ascend the organizational ladder, they must be given a range of opportunities to prepare them for the increasing responsibilities of strategic management. These opportunities may be as informal as having top management use the organization's strategy as a means for questioning product and market recommendations. Or, they may be more formal. For example, organizations with a decentralized structure can provide managers with hands-on experience in setting strategy by giving them the opportunity to set and implement the strategy of their unit, using corporate Mission Statements as a guide.

Providing opportunities for strategic thinking is important, but equally important is testing whether an individual has the inclination and capacity for strategic involvement. What must be developed is a way to measure this capacity. The recent research done on the human brain helps improve our understanding of the kind of mental attributes that predispose individuals toward strategic thinking. For example, the right hemisphere of the brain, with its intuitive, creative and holistic qualities, may, with some simplification, be called the strategic side of the brain. From our experience, the following characteristics are important indicators of high potential for strategic management.

- Conceptual thinking—the ability to think incisively and systematically about abstract categories such as basic beliefs and the decision-making process.

- Holistic viewpoint—the ability to see whole pictures without being confused or constrained by any of the parts.
- Expressiveness—the ability to translate abstract thinking about the organization into clear pictures that can be understood by others.
- Concern for the future—willingness to consider the future as an important dimension of management time and willingness to evaluate change or options.
- Tolerance for ambiguity—the ability to function effectively in situations of less than perfect information.
- A sense of stewardship—an inclination toward sacrificing short-run gain in order to protect the organization's resources and pass them on in better shape than they were in when received.

Once the capacity for strategic thinking is acknowledged to be necessary, we can be responsive to these questions: How do you improve the organization's ability to identify managers who are more "right brain" in their thinking? How do we develop their career path through the organization? What kinds of experiences are needed to develop these strategic qualities in operationally astute "left brain" managers, those who tend to be more logical, systematic and rational in their orientation?

To have meaning, giving appropriate strategic experiences to managers and then assessing their ability to handle those experiences must be accompanied by a re-evaluation of the reward system. To what extent are managers rewarded for strategic accomplishment? For example, for willingness to emphasize or de-emphasize a particular product or market for strategic considerations, without regard to immediate operational "pluses"; for willingness to modify or upgrade the human and physical capabilities they control for strategic as well as operational considerations; for unwillingness to develop a long-range plan without a clear notion of strategy.

Revamping the reward system to accommodate strategic accomplishment poses a number of difficulties. First, given the often-extended time horizon of strategy, it may not always be easy to fit reward for strategic accomplishment into a system skewed more toward recognition for annual results. This means that an effort must be made to translate strategy into specific action steps, so that the annual results against which managers are evaluated and rewarded include both strategic and operational elements.

A second difficulty arises from the tendency in most organizations to relate rewards to operational growth. Growth is essential to every organization, but over what period? Growth over time may entail reshuffling or even dismembering particular products or markets to fit future strategy. From this perspective, a manager who, following the strategy, successfully winds down an operation may contribute as much to "growth" as one who has had an outstanding year helping the business to grow operationally.

For years, "people" were said to be the most important asset of an organization. Yet, only recently has top management begun to take back the responsibility for the overall development of an organization's human resources. This is encouraging, given the need to strategically develop these resources. Knowing more about the kinds of strategic experiences that should be provided key managers, knowing how to assess the ability to think strategically, knowing how the reward system can be made responsive to strategic accomplishment, and knowing how to obtain and develop the skills required by a new Driving Force are all new and critical dimensions of top management's challenge in the human resource equation.

CHALLENGE: DETERMINING THE FUNCTION OF THE LONG-RANGE PLANNER IN STRATEGY FORMULATION

Given the separation between strategy and long- and short-range planning, the question arises: What role, if any, should the organization's planning function play in regard to strategy setting? More specifically, what are the strategic responsibilities of the corporate planner? There are at least two possible answers.

It can be argued in a somewhat hard-line fashion that planning should have no formal role to play in the area of strategy other than to understand it. Having separated strategy and planning at the conceptual level, an organization may continue the logic and separate the two functionally. Thus, the planning function would assist line management with operational planning and a strategic function could be developed that would help the top team set the strategic direction. And never the two functions shall meet.

There is at least one major drawback to this approach. To functionally separate strategy from planning is to risk having the planning department develop systems to generate projections, plans and budgets independently of the organization's strategy, or to have a strategy which is not really guiding day-to-day operations.

On the other hand, it can be argued—and we think more persuasively—that planning can and should play a role in the strategy area. Here, the key challenge becomes determining how to upgrade the planning function to accommodate its strategic responsibility, without compromising the strategy.

In meeting this challenge, a clear separation must be made between the responsibility of top management to set strategy and the role of planning as a facilitator in implementing strategy. This separation must be understood by both top managers and the planning staff.

One CEO drove home the point by having his senior planner participate in the top team's strategy session. Right at the start, the CEO made it clear to the group that it is "top management's responsibility—and ultimately mine—to determine our strategy. We own the content. The director of planning is here primarily to gain a full understanding of the strategy. This will help him to better carry out his main responsibility—facilitating the implementation of the strategy we set." The planner's presence at the meeting not only helped to delineate his responsibilities but also served to increase his credibility with the top team and with managers throughout the organization.

Making the planning function a responsive, willing ally of strategy is a key challenge. It requires carefully redirecting and shaping the planning function so that it can support the top team's strategic efforts.

CHALLENGE: SETTING UP TO INFLUENCE THE ENVIRONMENT

Environmental scanning is an important aspect of strategic thinking. In carefully setting future strategy, top management must identify, organize and use environmental data to define and test possible future Driving Forces. The need to improve the quality, accuracy and timeliness of information about the economy, technology, socio-political factors and competitors, and to have that information used by top management for setting strategy was the point about the environment made in our previous chapter on Critical Issues.

Beyond the cluster of Critical Issues surrounding environmental scanning, there remains a major challenge which cuts to the very survival of an organization. That challenge is: how can top management influence the shape of those environmental trends and events which are likely to have an impact on the Driving Force, the Strategic Framework and, consequently, the nature and direction of the business?

New approaches are required. Many of the standard, classic corporate messages for coping with and influencing the environment no longer work. The impact of the famous or infamous comment, "What's good for General Motors . . ." still lingers. The power of business to influence those groups that are playing key roles in initiating or conditioning environmental change is not altogether obvious. Government increasingly regulates the system. Consumer groups and environmentalists champion their causes. The young bring new values and troubling questions. The news media often project insensitivity and one-sidedness.

Debate and discussion have always been the catalysts for progress. That is as it should be. Given the profound importance of environmental questions, free and open exchange of ideas is absolutely essential. But business must become a more effective participant in these debates so its interests and point of view are reflected in the outcomes.

Having a clear strategy is not enough. Senior management must become more skilled at diagnosing relevant emerging environmental trends and more serious about clarifying the organization's stance on what constitutes a desired outcome. For example, as the public sector grows in importance, strategic managers must become more familiar with the inner workings of the political mind and the dynamics of the political decision-making process. To influence outcomes, one must understand how those outcomes are formulated. Otherwise, the organization's influence will be entrusted to public relations people, lobbyists and the good will of public officials. And top management actions will be limited to reacting after-the-fact to the inevitable downturns in that good will.

CHALLENGE: HOLDING THE INTERNATIONAL ORGANIZATION TOGETHER

Whether or not your organization calls itself a multinational, once your business extends beyond domestic borders you face the difficult task of forging a sense of unity from a situation which, almost by definition, increasingly lacks cohesion. Just about every organization engaged in international activity is confronted with managing the centrifugal forces implied by geographic distance, cultural diversity and dissimilar markets.

Regardless of the type and form of international involvement— wholly owned subsidiary, joint venture, international division, geographical or product line organization—overseas operations are becoming increasingly important. One reason for this is the contribution of these operations to the overall health of the organization. "Most major U.S. corporations," *Forbes* noted, "depend on their operations overseas for an astonishingly large proportion of their sales and, in most instances, an even larger portion of their profits." *

When the international aspect of an organization's activities increases in importance, it also grows in complexity. Truly global companies are evolving. For example, responding to sales market pressures, General Motors is becoming a "world company." As *Forbes* explained:

> The old auto market called for one car in Europe, say, and another for the U.S. The new auto market, with its emphasis on fuel efficiency, calls for a car that combines European economy with American comfort and convenience. A world car, in short. To produce it, GM is turning itself into a world company.
>
> . . . GM will be spending between $10 billion and $13 billion in the car wars of the eighties. An engine plant in Australia, a battery plant in France, an assembly plant in Mexico, a radio components plant in Singapore . . .

---

* James Cook, "A Game Any Number Can Play," *Forbes*, June 25, 1979, p. 50.

From such far-flung outposts, GM hopes to put together the center-piece of its strategy: a world car, blending U.S. and foreign design, that can be built with few changes, for any market.*

The sheer breadth and magnitude of the evolving global organization prohibits a neo-colonialist management style, one in which executives in the mother country control the action. Increasingly, equal opportunity demands are being made by indigenous managers. With first-rate business education, superb technical skills and with greater contribution being made to the organization's balance sheet, these managers are asking—and getting—key decision-making responsibility.

All this puts a premium on having a clear sense of direction. For strategic managers in a "world organization," several challenges must be addressed. What overall strategy will allow us to make maximum impact worldwide? What structure will best insure that we continue as a world organization? How do we shape the top management team so that its composition is as global as our strategy? How do we keep the widely dispersed business units focused on the corporate strategy?

CHALLENGE: TO SET STRATEGY WHEN YOU DON'T HAVE CORPORATE CLOUT

Let's assume you are a manager who heads a line division in a multinational organization. Even more specifically, your division is far removed from corporate headquarters. As you look toward the future, you realize that your organizational unit has been primarily guided by its long-range planning, within financial guidelines from the top. You are hesitant to use your past and present experience as your major guide to the changing future. Beyond these thoughts, you have never really been sure of the product and market limits or of how much flexibility you have. One thing, however, seems clear. Your product, market and resource thinking invariably gets accepted or shot down on operational grounds. As you further con-

* Bob Tamarkin, "GM Gets Ready for the World Car," *Forbes,* April 2, 1979, p. 44.

template where your division is headed, you begin to raise strategic questions: Given the distinctive features of the environment in which we operate and the competitive pressures we face, how will we make sure our unit will survive? What is our current Driving Force and what should it be? How would this alter the scope and priority of products, markets and resources required?

As you open next year's long-range planning package, you hear yourself asking, "What should I do?" There are several options. You might forget the strategic questions and get on with the job of long-range planning as you always have. You can also raise similar questions up front in your next plan, hoping to give some guidance to your plan and to stimulate interest among those reviewing your work.

A more exciting option is for you and your colleagues to formulate a strategy for your unit. In so doing, you will undoubtedly have to make certain assumptions about the corporate strategy. These must be subsequently tested with whoever has responsibility for review and approval. Even if your strategy statement does not survive the review process, an important victory has been won. You have laid the basis for a rational discussion about the strategic direction of your unit. And it is not inconceivable that your initiative will spark a chain reaction, prompting the larger organization to go about the task of setting strategy.

It is difficult to develop a line or staff unit strategy in the absence of a corporate one. Meeting this challenge may require as much artful diplomacy as it does skill at setting strategy. It also requires a level of maturity in the management structure of the organization. Those who review such a strategic initiative must think through the larger organizational strategy before they are quick to shoot down —or acclaim—such efforts.

CHALLENGE: KNOWING WHEN TO KICK AND WHEN TO NURTURE THE SACRED COWS

Psychologists tell us that beneath the conscious life of all human beings lies a realm which is remote and at least partially hidden from our perception. In this, organizations and the human organism are analogous. While organizations may not really have a collective unconscious, beneath the pattern of strategic and operational decision making there is an area of implicitly held beliefs, of tacit understanding about what should and should not be done, of unarticulated values that can influence the strategic direction of the organization. This is the area where the organization's sacred cows tend to roam.

A company we know is in the food business. It makes a line of premium products which are sold through supermarkets. While setting its strategy, this organization explored several Driving Forces, one of which was MARKET NEEDS. The organization enjoyed an excellent relationship with its distributors, even though it had traditionally refused to be coaxed into meeting a wider range of their needs. A MARKET NEEDS Driving Force would keep distributors happy. It would also require taking on several new products through sub-contractor arrangements.

As the discussion on strategy unfolded, it became clear that the MARKET NEEDS Driving Force ran counter to a belief that was never explicitly stated but, nevertheless, exercised great power over management decisions. This company always operated on the assumption that unless an organization grows, produces and packages a product on its own, it was just not right to sell it. Selling something that was not "yours" from start to finish was considered slightly illegitimate. Once the belief was explicitly stated, its meaning could be examined and its implications could be traced. As it turned out, few of the managers were willing to continue in a belief that however valid originally, had long outlived its usefulness. A sacred cow well kicked!

In one sense, implicit beliefs act as a kind of social cement which help to keep the organization together. Yet, because these beliefs can have a hidden influence on important strategic decisions, they must be examined rigorously. It may turn out that some sacred cows are, indeed, sacred. To make them explicit is to enable them to serve as a support for the Driving Force and Strategic Framework as the initial screen for major operational decisions. The CEO's lead in identifying an organization's implicitly held beliefs, getting them out on the table, setting aside those that have outlived their usefulness, and nurturing those that are strategically significant is a thoughtful challenge.

CHALLENGE: COMING TO TERMS WITH "STRATEGY BEYOND STRATEGY"

Put yourself in the following situation. About two years ago, your top team set the organization's strategy. It settled on a five-year time frame, given product life cycles and the rate of technological change in your industry. While implementation efforts are proceeding pretty much as planned, you begin to ask a few questions. "What happens when the current strategy runs its course?" "Even though our strategy is updated annually, shouldn't we take a longer-range view of our strategic requirements beyond the current strategic time frame?" "What, if anything, should we be doing now to make sure the action we take within our current strategy does not straitjacket the longer-term future?"

These are important and difficult questions. One reason they are so difficult is that most of us have little experience in answering them. One company has spent considerable time trying to come to terms with these questions. Their experience is worth recounting.

The top management team of this company met and assumed that the current strategy would remain pretty much intact through five years, the end of the time frame of the current strategy. An operational snapshot of the organization was taken, outlining the products, markets, resources, size, growth, return and structure that would characterize the organization, given the full implementation of its strategy over the five years. Considerable time was then spent examining a range of internal and external environmental inputs of consequence to the organization, projected ten years beyond the current strategic time frame. Finally, the managers asked a number of questions: Given these internal and external inputs, what should our strategy be for the ten years following our current five-year strategy? Assuming we continue to implement our current strategy, will that strategy be a good springboard upon which to launch our longer-term strategic efforts? Do we foresee conflict between the current and future strategies? What actions can we take now and in the next few years to insure that our current strategy is supportive of the strategy beyond it?

This organization found several major decisions that had to be made to more effectively position it for the longer-range strategy.

While every organization should explore "flying in front of the plane," some particular circumstances can make setting "strategy beyond strategy" absolutely essential.

- Your organization is dependent on a scarce resource with a limited life cycle.
- You know that at some point in the future your products run the risk of being eliminated by governmental legislation.
- Your customers are working to eliminate your products.
- Your products require a capital or labor intensity that, in the long run, most likely may be intolerable.
- Your products require a certain skill that is not likely to be readily available in the future.

The real challenge is to take the time and put the effort into grappling with a much longer-range "strategy beyond strategy." This is particularly difficult when you consider that some members of the top management team will not be around to contribute to its modification or implementation.

CONCLUSION

In fashioning a framework to guide the key choices that confront an organization, top managers exercise their ultimate power as decision makers. But this power carries a price tag. Strategy must be carefully and systematically formulated, Critical Issues must be resolved and important challenges need to be addressed.

Is reaching the goal of strategic effectiveness worth the effort? The chief executives we know feel it is. They voice an increasing sense of urgency about the importance of clear strategic thinking and about their own role in the strategy-setting process. And they know that for this urgency to be translated into effective action, top management must devote its most serious and incisive thinking to every facet of strategic management. In fact, why not start now? What is *your* organization's Driving Force? What are the consequences of continuing that Driving Force? What should your future Driving Force be? . . .

Organizing to Set Strategy

We have covered in detail the need for organizations to be guided by a clear statement of strategy. This need grows more and more acute. Today's organizations face a combined challenge from a less-than-bountiful environment, from competition which is world-wide in scope and often new in form, and from phenomena and trends which seem to defy the logic of our econometric models. For the first time, organizations are in danger of losing control over where they are headed. As we pointed out earlier, government, trade unions, interest groups, financial institutions—you name it— may have more impact on the direction of an organization than a top team which has been remiss in its obligation to set strategy.

If setting strategy continues to be critically important, it also remains exceedingly difficult. This difficulty is not a function of labor intensity or the time required to set strategy. Rather, the nature of strategy itself poses a difficulty. Strategy deals with ends, not means; with what the concept of the business is and should become. To formulate strategy is to make a judgment about the organization's reason for being. Such judgments are always difficult to make and even more difficult to test. How do you "prove" that yours is the "best" strategy?

Another difficulty is the elusiveness of the future dimension of time in which strategy runs its course. Considered from the present, "the future" does not actually exist. In fact, the expression is

115

merely a convenient shorthand to express the possible *futures* that lie before us. The future, in other words, is open-ended and indeterminate. And, if this is so, how do you know what information and experience is relevant for the future? And how can that information be organized so possible future strategies can be formulated, tested and narrowed to a final choice?

One other difficulty deserves mention: Many managers simply do not know how to set strategy. This is not because these managers lack capability or competence. Far from it. Rather, most organizations lack what can be called a tradition of strategic thinking. There is no significant reservoir of formalized experience that can be tapped to enable managers to gain the needed strategy skills. If they inquire about strategy, they will most likely be given the tools of long-range planning. Or, they might be pointed in the direction of the "entrepreneurial" CEO who has superb strategic instincts, but who knows little about how his own flashes of insight come about, much less being able to tell others how to become equally well endowed.

While it makes little sense to minimize these difficulties, it makes even less sense to become unnerved by them. Since managers must set strategy, they have little choice but to overcome whatever roadblocks may stand in their way. And the difficulties can be surmounted. We have found that a carefully organized approach is the best way to meet, head on, the difficulties posed by strategy setting. Using our experience as a reference point, let us look at some of the key elements that make for success in formulating strategy.

1. *Have the right people involved.* Regardless of the organization's size, strategy setting is a task for a relatively small group. Typically, no more than eight to twelve key managers participate. At the corporate level, the executive committee or management committee of most organizations would be the group to set strategy. Beyond the top management team, there may be exceptional circumstances under which a few additional participants may be considered. For example, a key board member whose buy-off is necessary; a unique information source whose input is needed; a key implementer whose commitment is vital; or, one or more members of the "second team" who can benefit from the experience. As

the number of participants increases, setting strategy becomes more difficult to undertake, and there may be no corresponding increase in the quality of output.

At the most general level, the "right people" are those whose thinking, judgment and counsel command the respect of the CEO or the top manager in the unit that is setting strategy. The top man must have confidence in the direction they help set. Chemistry is equally important. The group that sets strategy must be one in which the CEO can freely bare his soul. He must be comfortable enough to be candid.

2. *Have a process.* The word "process" has a variety of meanings and usages. People speak of the engineering process, the manufacturing process, the governing process, the process of growth and decay. All of these usages are, no doubt, valid. But we mean something very distinct when we talk about "a process." To us, a process is a necessary sequence of steps by which information and judgments are organized so that a conclusion can be reached. More specifically, to set strategy via a process is to set an organization's direction by an approach which is *rational, selective* and *universal.* Let us briefly examine each of these elements separately.

When we say that a process is *rational* we mean that it follows a logical, step-by-step approach. Information is organized and analyzed in a particular order or sequence, leading progressively to some overall conclusion. This means that strategy setting proceeds sequentially through a number of steps: determining the current Driving Force; developing possible future Driving Forces; selecting a future Driving Force and developing the Strategic Framework; identifying Critical Issues necessary for implementation.

The second attribute of a process is that it is *selective.* A process for setting strategy must include a set of questions that uncovers the relevant information necessary to complete each step in the process and to zone off the irrelevant.

The third attribute of a process is its *universality.* A process is independent of the particular content to which it is applied. It is the organizing princille of data and thinking and, therefore, remains constant.

A process to set strategy must accomplish two important results. First, it must bring out the intuitive, unarticulated "sense" of direction successful top managers carry with them. A strategic process must capitalize on such instincts and make them explicit so they can be critically examined. It must start where managers are.

Second, a strategic process must answer the question: Where should the organization be headed? Strategy is formulated in the present, but designed for the future. Consequently, it is based not only upon information—facts—about the present, but judgments about the future. Strictly speaking, there are no future "facts," only educated guesses —judgments—as to what the facts will be and what the implications are for an organization's strategy. A strategic process, therefore, must focus on getting out, defining and testing judgments about the organization's future, so that a coherent framework emerges which can be communicated and which can guide operational planning and decision making. For us, the concept of Driving Force is key to using information and judgment to fashion a Strategic Framework for the organization.

To sum up: Unless you organize strategy setting around a conscious approach or "process," you will be unable to proceed systematically toward a sound conclusion. A process does not guarantee success, but at the very least it enables you to reconstruct the logic behind your conclusions. If your efforts are successful, that success becomes repeatable. If your strategy fails, you will be able to pinpoint why. And, if significant new information forces you to reevaluate the strategy, you will know how to use that information to make whatever adjustments may be necessary without the typical panic of starting over.

3. *Know your end results.* Any activity as complicated as setting strategy requires a clear definition of anticipated results. The results of applying the process of strategy formulation we have discussed are:
   • A clear statement of strategy that can be easily retained.
   • A shared understanding and commitment among top managers to this common direction.

- A vehicle for communicating strategy throughout the organization.
- An approach to implementing and managing the strategy.
- A basis for simplifying and managing long- and short-range planning.
- An understanding of the strategy process that can be reapplied.

4. *Getting the job done.* Top management's interest and involvement in the formulation of strategy must always be directed against the end results: a clear and useful statement of strategy which guides those choices that determine the nature and direction of an organization; a way to manage that strategy; and the supporting documentation that led to the conclusion. In working with top management, we have been primarily concerned with providing a process to guide its strategic deliberations and a structure to efficiently apply that process. This process and structure include:

Prework

Each participant provides an assessment of the key internal and external factors which will be used to set future strategy. For example, environmental threats and opportunities, unique strengths, basic beliefs, competition.

Working session

The top team meets to articulate current strategy, to use the prework information to develop possible future Driving Forces and to narrow those to a tentative future Driving Force and Strategic Framework.

Follow-on

Individual and small group reflection, review and sharpening of the tentative future Driving Force and Strategic Framework, within a prescribed format.

Follow-up working session

The top team regroups to further develop and complete the future Strategic Framework, to test and challenge that

Framework, to identify Critical Issues, and to develop a plan to manage that strategy and those Critical Issues.

Reviews

A six-month review of problems and progress and a one-year detailed review and update of the strategy, including setting "strategy beyond strategy."

A note on time

Four or five working days over a two-month period are required to set strategy. Two or three working days are required for the review and one-year update of strategy.

A final word

The CEO, chairman or division head, whoever is ultimately responsible for the strategy of the organization or unit being considered, plays the pivotal role. Only with his full commitment and active participation in every aspect of strategic management will strategy be set and used to guide the major decisions that confront the organization.

Selected
Annotated
Bibliography

Ackoff, Russell L. *A Concept of Corporate Planning*. New York: Wiley-Interscience, 1970.

A philosophy of planning is presented focusing more on the objectives and logic of the planning process than on planning techniques. The author distinguishes "strategic planning" from "tactical planning," the former being "long-range corporate planning that is ends-oriented (but not exclusively so)." He finds the differences between the two more "relative" than we would care to admit. Three philosophies of planning are analyzed: 'satisficing', optimizing and adaptivizing. The latter represents a new planning concept requiring scientific methods, tools and techniques. Planning is divided into five "parts," including: ends—specificiation of objectives and goals; means—selection of policies, programs, etc.; resources—determining needs, and how they can be attained and allocated; implementation—carrying out the plan, control—design of a procedure for anticipating or detecting and correcting failures in the plan. Each of these "parts" is analyzed in depth.

Andrews, Kenneth R. *The Concept of Corporate Strategy*. Homewood, Illinois: Dow Jones-Irwin, Inc., 1971.

Strategy is defined as the "pattern of major objectives, purposes, or goals and essential policies and plans for achieving those goals, stated in such a way as to define what business a company is in or is to be in and the kind of company it is or is to be." While this definition encompasses a "how" element, the author's subsequent discussion separates the formulation of strategy from its implementation. The "general manager's" task is viewed in terms of four functions: supervising current operations, planning future operations, coordinating the functions and human capabilities of the organization, and making a distinctive personal contribution. Tying these functions together is the primary job of the general manager: supervising the process for formulating, refining and realizing the organization's strategy. The book offers a careful examination of the constituent elements of strategy and outlines the requirements for successful implementation.

Ansoff, Igor H. *Corporate Strategy.* New York: McGraw-Hill Book Company, 1965.

A comprehensive "strategic decision theory" is offered. The book is directed toward managers ranging from the chairman of the board to the development and planning staff. The central challenge of any business is how "to configure and direct the resource conversion process in such a way as to optimize the attainment of the objectives." This, in turn, requires three categories of decisions: strategic, administrative and operative. Strategic decisions deal with the relations between the firm and the environment, particularly with the selection of product mix and markets. This thoughtful work examines the major steps of strategy formulation: objectives setting; internal and external appraisal of the firm; assessment of the firm's competencies and shortcomings; and the formulation of a strategy for action.

Ansoff, Igor H. *Strategic Management.* New York: John Wiley and Sons, 1979.

A "managerial theory" is proposed which attempts to answer such questions as: What are the patterns of organizational behavior in a turbulent environment? What determines the differences in the behavior? What factors contribute to success and to failure? What determines the choice of a particular mode of behavior? What is the transition process by which organizations move from one mode to another? The author develops a five-point scale of turbulence, the same scale for different types of response, and the same scale for the organizational culture and capability for response. An organization will be successful if environment, response, culture and capability match each other. The focus throughout is on strategic behavior of organizations—the process of interaction with the environment—together with changing "internal configurations and dynamics." The author borrows from a wide range of disciplines, including logic, politics, sociology, psychology and information science, to produce a rigorously stated "applied theory" designed to help diagnose and improve the behavior of organizations in the public and private sectors.

Ansoff, H. I., Declerck, R. P., & Hayes, R. L., eds. *From Strategic Planning to Strategic Management.* London: John Wiley and Sons, 1976.

A book of wide-ranging articles focusing primarily on the interaction between the organization's capabilities and strategy. Its approach is multi-disciplinary. There is a tendency toward abstract discussion, so read selectively. Some articles attempt to construct a conceptual framework for strategic thinking; others relate to the "linkages" between the organization and the environment; still others explore the "strategy and structure" relationship. The sections on the changing role of the strategic manager and the education, selection and training of strategic managers shed light on an important but often neglected area of strategic management.

Argenti, John. *Systematic Corporate Planning*. London: Nelson, 1974.

The philosophy and the technology of planning are comprehensively described. Corporate planning is a systematic approach to clarify corporate objectives, make strategic decisions and check the progress of those decisions. Strategic decisions affect or are intended to affect the organization as a whole over long time periods. The key distinction between strategic planning and other planning is said to be the corporate nature of strategic planning. We would say that the key distinction lies elsewhere. The author suggests analyzing strengths, weaknesses, opportunites and threats, and offers a variety of techniques for assessing information in these areas. The charts, graphs and matrices help the author make his points; the case-study material illustrates and illuminates the discussion.

Bower, Marvin. *The Will to Manage*. New York: McGraw-Hill Book Company, 1966.

The management task is viewed not simply in terms of achieving economic results through operating decisions but as developing "managing processes" by which all members of the organization can contribute to achieving its objectives. The best way to translate the "will" to manage into effective management action is through "programmed management" —a systems approach by which top managers build their own management system fitted to the nature and needs of the organization. Fourteen basic management processes are delineated, among which are: setting objectives, planning strategy, establishing goals, developing a company philosophy. While strategy and long-range planning are "not synonymous," the author tends to mix the two. The book's major strength is its perceptive commentary on the basic management processes and the wealth of examples drawn from firsthand consulting experience.

Chandler, Alfred D., Jr. *Strategy and Structure: Chapters in the Economic History of the American Industrial Enterprise*. Cambridge, Massachusetts: The M.I.T. Press, 1962.

This book presents an investigation into the changing strategy and structure of the large industrial enterprise in the United States. Using the comparative method of analysis, the author shows how seventy of the largest corporations in America have adapted their structures to meet the demands of the expanding business. The major portion of the work is devoted to the administrative histories of four companies: du Pont, General Motors, Standard Oil (New Jersey) and Sears, Roebuck. It demonstrates how their innovative use of the "decentralized" form of organization evolved as each company expanded and diversified. Strategy is defined as the "determination of the basic long-term goals and objectives of an enterprise, and the adoption of courses of action and the allocation of resources necessary for carrying out these goals." While we would quarrel with this definition, the author ably shows how an organization's strategy and the organizational form necessary to support that strategy are intimately linked, and how executives who make operational decisions independent of a clear sense of strategy have failed to carry out their roles in the economy and in their firms.

Ewing, David W., ed. *Long-Range Planning for Management*. New York: Harper and Row, 1964.

This ground-breaking compendium is a *tour de force* of ideas about long-range planning by such authors as Peter Drucker, George Steiner, H. Igor Ansoff, and others. The chapters on the "Nature and Principles" of long-range planning and on "Strategy" are particularly useful to managers interested in deepening their understanding of both tools.

Ferguson, Charles R. *Measuring Corporate Strategy*. Homewood, Illinois: Dow Jones-Irwin, Inc., 1974.

This book advances the view that a manager must be more concerned with "concepts" than with technology. The effective executive must deal with the design of the corporation. At some point, all organizations require basic changes. To evaluate those changes, the author suggests a "concept audit," which probes the major elements of the corporation: organization structure and systems, management—quality, style and compensation—resource allocation, interaction with the environment. The author proposes the formation of a Strategy Implementation Task Force which can clarify top management expectations about how the company should function and reveal differences in those expectations. Such differences must be resolved for reorganization to proceed smoothly. The book's major usefulness is in the battery of diagnostic questions it raises to get out the "concepts" behind each aspect of the organization.

Rothschild, William E. *Putting It All Together*. New York: Amacom, 1976.

A practical, comprehensive guide that presents a sequential and integrated approach to strategy development and review. Strategy is defined as "a statement of an organization's investment priorities, the management thrust, and the ways that it will use its strengths and correct its limitations to pursue the opportunities and avoid threats facing it." Quite a mouthful! Strategy comprises three types of strategic decisions, at three different levels: investment decisions, resources decisions and a specific set of programs describing how resources will be employed to build on strengths and correct limitations. The author carefully separates strategy formulation from strategy implementation and suggests specific methodologies for accomplishing both tasks.

Rothschild, William E. *Strategic Alternatives*. New York: Amacom, 1979.

This book focuses on stimulating the generation of strategic alternatives. It is written to help managers recognize the large number of strategic alternatives that have been successfully used, and to increase insight about these options—when they will and will not work, and what they will require to succeed. Thirty-seven different business strategies are discussed, illustrated and evaluated. The chapters on "implementation strategy" provide a means of translating "investment" and "management" strategies into functional strategies, and are, therefore, of particular interest to functional executives.

Smith, Theodore A. *Dynamic Business Strategy*. New York: McGraw-Hill, 1977.

This book defines strategy as "the plan for getting the best returns from resources, the selection of the kind of business to engage in, and the scheme for obtaining a favorable position in the business field." This is somewhat vague. Strategy is said to encompass three areas: "perspective strategy"—the investigation of the nature of market, industry and environmental structures and the development of informational tools for dealing with them; "optimizing strategy"—the process of fitting the organizational programs into the industry structure and the manner in which the resources can be utilized to maximum benefit; "prospective strategy"—a means for dealing with change either expected or unexpected and a plan for adjusting to new environmental developments. The author offers concrete steps to help minimize potential errors in formulating strategy.

Steiner, George A. *Strategic Planning*. London: Collier-Macmillan Publishers, 1979.

A comprehensive management guide that runs the gamut from strategy to long-range planning, to budgeting and control. While strategy formulation is an art, it can and should be formally approached. Checklists, matrices and charts are provided to convert that art to a more practical science. The author draws a distinction between strategy and tactics. Strategy is the framework within which tactical moves are made. Tactics implement strategy. Substrategies of production, marketing, finance and personnel are explored. Much space is devoted to discussing how strategy can be implemented.

Steiner, George A. *Top Management Planning*. London: Collier-Macmillan Limited, 1969.

This monumental undertaking of more than seven hundred pages approaches planning from "top management's" point of view. This puts the book's focus on "strategic planning," and not "tactical planning." Planning is defined as "reasoning about how a business will get where it wants to go. Indeed, a basic task of comprehensive planning is to visualize the business as the managers wish it to be in the future." Putting the "what" and "how" under the planning umbrella gives us concern. The book's major strengths are its comprehensiveness and its helpful prescriptive motif: many planning practices that have been successfully used are highlighted.

Warren, E. Kirby. *Long-Range Planning.* Englewood Cliffs, New Jersey: Prentice-Hall, Inc., 1966.

This is a succinct analysis of long-range planning which seeks to critically evaluate and improve the current state of the art and the practice of planning. It accomplishes both objectives handily. The book assesses the importance of long-range planning both to individual corporations and to the national economic position of the United States, defining what planning is and outlining the roadblocks to effective planning. Of particular interest is the discussion on developing better ways to measure and evaluate the quality of plans and planning efforts.

About the Authors

BENJAMIN B. TREGOE is Chairman of the Board and Chief Executive Officer of Kepner-Tregoe, Inc., an international management, education and organization development firm located in Princeton, New Jersey.

Dr. Tregoe received his B.A. from Whittier College and his Ph.D. in sociology from Harvard University. He has lectured and published extensively throughout the world.

While he was serving as a social scientist with the Rand Corporation in Santa Monica, California, from 1955 to 1958, he and his colleague, Charles H. Kepner, Ph.D., became aware of the critical need that managers have for a logical method for solving problems and making decisions. These two scientists resigned from Rand and devoted their time to developing a systematic approach to problem solving, decision making and planning.

Out of this collaboration grew Kepner-Tregoe, Inc., a firm which today employs 200 people worldwide. Over the past 20 years, this corporation has been responsible for transferring its systematic problem-solving and decision-making processes to more than 1,000,000 participants in 14 languages and in 44 countries. Dr. Tregoe is coauthor with Dr. Kepner of *The Rational Manager,* a landmark book in the field of management methods.

JOHN W. ZIMMERMAN is Senior Vice President and a Director of Kepner-Tregoe, Inc., which he joined in 1961. His current responsibilities include new conceptual research and corporate business development. Over the last ten years he has specialized, along with

Dr. Benjamin Tregoe, in the development and delivery of Strategy Formulation, a program to help chief executive officers and their top teams determine the future direction of their organizations. It is from this work that the present book derives.

A native of Milwaukee, Wisconsin, Mr. Zimmerman received his B.S. degree from the University of Tennessee and his M.B.A. from the University of Wisconsin. He has served in industrial engineering with Oscar Mayer & Company and in production management and corporate training with the Pillsbury Company, has contributed articles on strategy and management development to a wide number of professional journals, and is an active guest speaker internationally for numerous business and professional groups. He is a continuing lecturer at Centre D'Etudes Industrielles (CEI) in Geneva, Switzerland.